W9-CEJ-408

"Provocative and challenging. Even when I find myself
disagreeing with Brian Godawa in his evaluation of a particular film,
his cinematé and sophisticated point of view command attention."

MICHAEL MEDVED, *film critic and*
author of **Hollywood Versus America**

"At last! A Christian book about Hollywood by a Hollywood Christian.
With biblical balance and artistic insight, Brian Godawa cautions
against both the legalisms of cultural anorexia and the naiveté of cultural gluttony. I'll
never again watch a movie and be content to simply say whether or not I liked it!
And Godawa's appendix on sex, violence and profanity in the Bible
promises to explode like a biblical bombshell among those
whose idea of cultural critique is merely counting fornications
on the silver screen. The appendix alone is worth its weight in gold!"

GREG JOHNSON, *resident theologian, St. Louis Center for Christian Study, and*
author of **The World According to God**

"The greatest special effect in any movie is a great story. Brian Godawa, a screenwriter
himself, understands this and understands the power in a good story's underlying
assumptions. His fine book is a helpful guide for everyone who likes to go to the movies
without checking their faith at the door."

PAUL SAILHAMER, *seminar instructor, Faith Goes to the Movies*

"This is an important book. Brian Godawa opens doors of understanding
that we never knew were there. He gives us a grid through which we can clearly see
what is going on philosophically and theologically within cinema art.
Very simply, Brian has written the best book on the various worldviews behind popular
Hollywood movies to date. I cannot recommend it enough."

DAVID BRUCE, *webmaster, HollywoodJesus.com*

"Brian's analysis is insightful and stimulating. Our biblical values are colliding
with worldviews in the movies, and Brian shows us why. Those values are also
illuminated by intersecting with movies, and I find that especially exciting.
We might even understand the Bible with more insight from seeing these connections.
The chapter on sex and violence is worth the price of the book.
What I appreciate the most is Brian's attention to detail, to a wide number of movie
examples, and his ability to simply frame the arguments of overused words
like *postmodern*. He doesn't talk about the surface issues from a country-club
Christian perspective but helps me discern what movies are about.
I appreciate the hard work he has done, and look forward to reading and
rewatching some of those movies again."

RALPH WINTER, *producer,* **Planet of the Apes, X-Men, Left Behind**

Hollywood Worldviews

Watching Films with Wisdom & Discernment

Brian Godawa

InterVarsity Press
Downers Grove, Illinois

InterVarsity Press
P.O. Box 1400, Downers Grove, IL 60515-1426
World Wide Web: www.ivpress.com
E-mail: mail@ivpress.com

InterVarsity Press® is the book-publishing division of InterVarsity Christian Fellowship/USA®, a student
movement active on campus at hundreds of universities, colleges and schools of nursing in the United States
of America, and a member movement of the International Fellowship of Evangelical Students. For
information about local and regional activities, write Public Relations Dept., InterVarsity Christian
Fellowship/USA, 6400 Schroeder Rd., P.O. Box 7895, Madison, WI 53707-7895, or visit the IVCF website
at <www.ivcf.org>.

Unless otherwise indicated, Scripture taken from the New American Standard Bible, © *1960, 1962, 1963,*
1968, 1971, 1972, 1973, 1975, 1977 by the Lockman Foundation. Used by permission.

Cover photograph: Erik Dreyer/Getty Images
ISBN 0-8308-2321-2
Printed in the United States of America ∞

Library of Congress Cataloging-in-Publication Data

Godawa, Brian.
    Hollywood worldviews: watching films with wisdom & discernment/Brian Godawa.
      p. cm.
    Includes bibliographical references.
    ISBN 0-8308-2321-2 (paper: alk. paper)
    1. Motion pictures—Religious aspects—Christianity. I. Title.

PN1995.5 .G65 2002
791.43'6823—dc21

                                                  2002023275

P	18	17	16	15	14	13	12	11	10	9	8	7	6	5	4	
Y	17	16	15	14	13	12	11	10	09	08	07	06	05	04	03	

To the memory of
Francis A. Schaeffer and H. R. Rookmaaker,
who both taught me to see
the worldview behind the art.

Contents

Preface

I am a screenwriter. I've been at it for over twelve years, winning various screenwriting contest honors and script options[1] along the way. I write stories that interest me, stories that move me, like the one I adapted for the feature film *To End All Wars.*[2] What I have to say about the craft and industry of filmmaking comes from my experience as a writer in the business.

Any movie that gets made is the result of a collaboration of hundreds of people. And they are all responsible in differing degrees for the final result of the film: its look, its feel, its visual, audible and dramatic impact. From the set designer to the cinematographer to the actors to the key grips and gofers, a movie would not be what it is without everyone involved in the process. Dozens of these individuals affect the content, from the writer to the director to the producer to the executives overseeing the project. No doubt each of these persons have unique perspectives on what is important in a film, but all would agree that the story is king. If you don't have a good story, you won't have a good movie, no matter who is acting in it or lighting it or directing it or producing it. If the story doesn't work, the movie doesn't work.

---

[1] A script option is when a producer or studio contracts for the rights to a script in order to consider making it into a movie. This is only the first step in the process; 99.9 percent of optioned scripts do not get made.

[2] *To End All Wars,* directed by David L. Cunningham and starring Kiefer Sutherland and Robert Carlyle, is based on Ernest Gordon's *Through the Valley of the Kwai* (New York: Harper, 1962), the true story of Allied POWs who suffered in the Burma-Siam prison camps under the Imperial Japanese during World War II and forced to build a railroad through hundreds of miles of man-eating jungle. At the time of this writing, *To End All Wars* has not yet been released in theaters. The website may be available for viewing at <www.toendallwars.com>.

It's the writer who crafts that story from the very beginning. Other people working on the film exercise their craft to bring to life the blueprint of something that already exists: the script. The writer alone must face the blank page and create *ex nihilo*—from nothing. Whether writing a "spec" script[3] or adapting someone else's book or idea, the writer must find the heart and soul of the story and capture it in dramatic narrative and dialogue. The story is where it all begins and ends. The lighting, cinematography, directing, acting, visual style . . . all are profoundly a part of the process, but they all serve the story—because the story is king. In this sense, all those participating in the production of a movie are storytellers, not merely the writer.

It is this primary importance of the story that originally drew me to the movies. There's just something about a good story that makes me sit up and listen: the captivation of narrative, the magnetism of drama, the curiosity of interesting characters and the meaning of it all. It's no wonder Jesus used parables and stories to make his points and explain the unexplainable nature of God's kingdom to his followers. A story enables us to understand a transcendent reality we may not otherwise have been able to grasp with mere rational abstraction. Drama brings to life the issues of life.

Great movies are like incarnate sermons. Watching sympathetic heroes work through their experiences often has more impact on my life than a rigorously reasoned abstract argument. Watching Eric Liddell run for God in *Chariots of Fire* proves to me that living for God without compromise is worth far more than what the world provides. Reliving the dilemmas of Captain John Miller and his men in *Saving Private Ryan* reminds me to be grateful for those who sacrificed for the precious freedom I enjoy. Both of these movies (and others) force me to reevaluate my life so that I don't squander it on self-seeking pettiness. I remember some movies better than most sermons, probably because they put flesh onto the skeleton of abstract ideas about how life ought or ought not be lived.

---

[3]A spec script is a screenplay that is written "on speculation," that is, without anyone's financial commitment, with the hope of being able to solicit interest in it *after* it is written.

That's why I got into movies and that's why I write about them now. From the funniest comedy to the saddest tragedy, movies capture the imagination, but they also convey the values and worldviews that we hold dear (as well as some we detest). My goal is to help the viewer discern those ideas that drive the story to its destination and how they influence us to live our lives—to understand the story *behind* the story.

I would like to thank the following for their help with hammering out this manuscript: my lovely wife, Kim, for all her patience and support; my graceful theologian, Ken Gentry; my transcendentally nimble philosopher, Aaron Bradford; my amusing and forbearing editor, David Zimmerman; my writing pal and sister-in-law, Shari Risoff; my movie buddies, Eric and Laura Baesel; a mighty warrior of the pen, Tal Brooke; a mighty CRI editor and movie buff, Melanie Cogdill; CRI's research monster, Stephen Ross; the storymeister, Jim Womer; my lifelong friend, Rich Knox; and as always—Joe.

And a very special thanks to Internet Movie Database <www.imdb.com> for its indispensable information on movie stats.

Introduction

"Movies corrupt the values of society."

"Too much sex and violence."

"They're worldly and a waste of time."

Those are just a few of the refrains repeated by many of today's culturally concerned Americans. Our cultural psyche has been damaged by Hollywood's defiant decadence and its relentless pushing of the envelope of common decency. But such sentiments suffer from a diluted mixture of truth and error. Not only do they miss the positive values that *do* exist in many movies, but also those who would completely withdraw from culture because of its imperfection suffer a decreasing capacity to interact redemptively with that culture. They don't understand the way people around them think because they are not familiar with the "language" those people are speaking or the culture they are consuming. A communication barrier results, and these cultural abstainers often end up in irrelevance and alienation from others. I call these artistic teetotalers *cultural anorexics.*

But the cultural anorexics also endanger their own humanity. The arts (of which movies are a part) are a God-given means of expressing our humanity. The creation of art, though flawed or imperfect, reflects the creativity and beauty of our Creator. To reject any of the arts *in toto* is to reject the *imago Dei,* the image of God in humanity. Even though we are fallen, with our art partaking of this fallenness, we are still created in the image of God, and therefore our creations continue to reflect our Maker.

As Francis Schaeffer was fond of pointing out, that image comes through even if the artist tries to suppress it. This is so because all truth is, in one sense, God's truth, no matter who is saying it, be he prophet, infidel or donkey.

Sometimes the most egregious lies are expressed through so-called Christian culture. For instance, dramatic pulpit oratory too often is infected by heresy, and public testimony too often panders to sensationalism. Christian movies, though well intentioned and sincere, often suffer from heavy-handedness in their desire to convert the unbeliever through art. Rather than being true to the ambiguities and difficulties of reality, rather than wooing the viewer with the right questions, an emphasis on answers often results in preachiness and a tendency toward platitudes. Authenticity and integrity can suffer because of manipulation. Which is more to be avoided: a pagan movie that rings true or "Christian" propaganda that rings false?

But another individual occupies the opposite end of the spectrum, and this one I call the *cultural glutton.* This is the person who consumes popular art too passively, without discrimination. Here are some of the expressions common to the cultural glutton:

"I just want to be entertained."

"You shouldn't take it so seriously."

"It's only a movie."

Cultural gluttons prefer to avoid analyzing movies beyond their entertainment value. They just want to escape and have fun for two hours in another world. When challenged by cultural critics to discern the messages within the movies, these moviegoers balk at such criticism as being too analytical or "reading into things." And many filmmakers mouth agreement with them.

One of Samuel Goldwyn's most famous sayings is "If you want to send a message, use Western Union." The meaning of this maxim is that movies are for entertainment, not the transmission of personal, political, social or religious views. And many share this viewpoint. No less a screenwriting icon than William Goldman (author of *The Princess Bride* and screenwriter of *Misery*) has pronounced, "Movies are finally, centrally, crucially, primarily *only* about story."[1]

Conventional wisdom and popular idols notwithstanding, nothing could be more of a half-truth. While it is true that story is the foundation of movies, an examination of the craft and structure of storytelling reveals that the drawing power of movies is not simply that they are "good stories" in some indefinable sense but that these stories are *about something*. They narrate the events surrounding characters who overcome obstacles to achieve some goal and who, in the process, are confronted with their personal need for change. In short, movie storytelling is about *redemption*—the recovery of something lost or the attainment of something needed.

I propose an amendment to Goldman's thesis that would complete the thought more accurately: Movies may be about story, but those stories are finally, centrally, crucially, primarily, *mostly* about redemption.[2]

Worldviews

Every religion and philosophy ultimately encompasses a worldview, a comprehensive web of beliefs through which we interpret our experiences—it is our *view* of the *world*. The simplest common denominator of all religious and philosophical worldviews is the belief that something is wrong with the world and there is some way to fix it.

Monists believe that everything in the universe is ultimately one in essence. Humanity is without peace because we falsely perceive distinctions among things. This perception of distinction is itself alienation. Humanity's redemption, according to the monist, is to change this perception so that we see all things as ultimately one. When we do so, we find the harmony we lack in our lives.

The rationalist philosopher believes that our problem stems from irra-

---

[1]William Goldman, *William Goldman: Four Screenplays* (New York: Applause, 1995), p. 2.

[2]Storytelling may have many functions, such as presenting historical information, providing moral teaching and offering a ritual or spiritual explanation. Depending on the kind of story, movies certainly may fulfill other purposes, but the redemptive aspect is, I believe, the dominant one.

tionality. If we would only align ourselves with logical principles, we would redeem ourselves from the irrationality of emotion and the unreliability of our senses.

The Christian worldview sees humanity as sinful and alienated from our Maker as well as from our fellow human beings, and this alienation exposes us to the inevitability of God's eternal wrath. Redemption in Christianity is found in the substitutionary sacrifice of the innocent (Christ) in place of the guilty (sinners), which pays the penalty of sin (justice) and reconciles the sinner to God and to others (mercy).

Worldviews are, of course, more complex than a mere paragraph of description. Someone who wants to understand the nuances that make up the existing worldviews should look beyond the limits of this book.

Director's Cut

For an introductory examination of worldviews, see James W. Sire, *The Universe Next Door: A Basic Worldview Catalog* (Downers Grove, Ill.: InterVarsity Press, 1997); and Norman L. Geisler and William Watkins, *Perspectives: Understanding and Evaluating Today's World Views* (San Bernardino, Calif.: Here's Life, 1984). Visit ‹www.godawa.com› for further reading on the basics.

The redemption in a particular worldview or belief system is its proposal for how to fix what is wrong with us. And redemption includes values about the way people ought or ought not to live and behave in this world. If a story is about a character who learns that lying hurts others and that family is more important than career (as in *Liar Liar* with Jim Carrey, 1997), then that story's redemptive message is that people's alienation is solved through honesty and family. We *ought* to make family and honesty more important than career and success. If a story is about clever, suave criminals getting away with a crime (as in *Ocean's 11*, 2001), the story's redemptive message, immoral though it may be, fits the perception of criminals: crime pays, and hipness is more important than obeying the law.

I will show in the following chapters that most movies follow a main character who seeks a specific goal and in so doing learns something about himself or herself and the world in a way that inevitably results in this person's redemption—or lack thereof.[3]

Suspension of Disbelief

We are all aware of the age-old question of whether art mirrors or influences society. Luminaries from both sides of the aisle have weighed in on the reflection/infection debate. And this debate will probably rage on till the Final Judgment. In his book *Hollywood Versus America,*[4] film critic and Hollywood bogeyman Michael Medved argues that filmmakers *intend* to influence the public through the values and characters they portray in television and film. His thoroughly documented opus concludes that entertainment reinforces certain values over others, namely those that reflect the current fashion of the creative community.

He points out the hypocrisy of those in the dream business who proclaim that movies don't influence belief or behavior while charging millions of dollars for advertising and product placements in movies and receiving awards and prestige for promoting trendy social agendas. His thesis is that since many movies do not reflect the dominant values of the American public, and often self-consciously defy financial interest, they can only be deliberate attempts by those involved to influence public opinion.

But it is also true that much entertainment meets an already existing demand in the audience. The public is not always consistent with its own claim of traditional morality. A herd instinct still guides the masses toward titillation of already darkened senses. Actions *do* speak louder

---

[3]Some critics of this view claim that redemption is an arbitrary theme. One could just as easily say that all movies are about sex; any movie that doesn't deal with sex is about the suppression of sex. But sex as an underlying theme is a Freudian novelty; a theology of storytelling comes from a more objective standard: the Bible. As I will discuss in later chapters, the nature of storytelling as narrative with a purpose and a view toward redemption is a presupposition of the Christian worldview. God, the author of history, tells fictional and nonfictional stories to show the meaning behind life and the possibility of redemption. Humankind, made in God's image, has told stories in this way since creation.

[4]Michael Medved, *Hollywood Versus America: Popular Culture and the War on Traditional Values* (New York: HarperCollins, 1992).

than words, as box office numbers so eloquently illustrate.

It is the position of this book that movies *both* reflect *and* influence society. An Oliver Stone film like *JFK* (1991) may be obvious in its intent to propagandize, but it is no less a reflection of what a certain segment of the population already believes. *Hannibal* (2001), the sequel to *Silence of the Lambs* (1991), may certainly push the moral envelope with a sympathetic cannibal as hero, but millions went to see it knowing full well what they were in for. A movie like that doesn't make well over $160 million at the box office by scandalously breaking new moral ground with an unwilling public. The ground is already tilled in the hearts of the people or they wouldn't want to see it. The success of *Hannibal* reflects a society already fascinated with evil.

While it is true that some movies may be more influential than others, it is incumbent upon moviegoers to understand what they are consuming and the nature of their amusement. It is not the least bit ironic that the word *amusement* means "without thought" (its original usage was "to delude or deceive"). Sadly, this is all too often what happens when the lights go down and the curtains go up. We suspend our disbelief and, along with it, our critical faculties.

By knowing something of the craft of storytelling, of its structure and nature, the average moviegoer might be less inclined to treat his or her viewing as mere entertainment and see it more for what it is: a means of communicating worldviews and values with a view toward redemption. This knowledge need not spoil the joy in entertainment or justify total withdrawal from culture. Rather, it can deepen one's appreciation and sharpen one's discernment. The goal of this education is to aid the reader in striking a balance between two extremes: cultural anorexia (rejecting all moviegoing because of any negative aspects) and cultural gluttony (consuming too many movies without discretion).

Authorial Intent and Reader Response

My personal involvement in movies dictates the focus of this book. I have decided to concentrate primarily on American mainstream movies made in the last fifteen years or so. The classics have much to offer in the way of analysis, but I am not as familiar with them, so they are for another to explore. This book also contains few references to foreign and art-house films, because these are not as widely viewed within the main-stream. You are welcome to consider this bias a weakness or a strength.

My goal in this book is to increase art appreciation. I want to inform the reader of the nature of storytelling and analyze how worldviews are communicated through most Hollywood movies, in order to aid the viewer's ability to discern the ideas being communicated. As readers sharpen their understanding of movies, they will be more capable of dis-cerning the good from the bad and avoid the extremes of cultural deser-tion (anorexia) and cultural immersion (gluttony).

The depiction of sex and violence in movies is a legitimate concern. I include an appendix at the end of the book that sets a foundation for mea-suring appropriateness in portrayals of vice in film, based on how the Bible deals with sex, violence and profanity. If you are particularly con-cerned about these issues, I suggest that you read the appendix first.

In the first part of the book, "Storytelling in the Movies," I lay some groundwork for discernment by discussing the nature of storytelling, including its mythological, theological and sociological aspects (chapter one) as well as the structural elements that screenwriters use to write their stories (chapter two). By learning how stories affect us and how screenwriters practice their craft, the lay audience can sharpen their art appreciation skills for movies and better discern how ideas are communi-cated through such storytelling.

In part two, "Worldviews in the Movies," I briefly introduce the preva-lent philosophies of existentialism (chapter three) and postmodernism (chapter four) so that the viewer can understand them when he or she sees them in current movies. In the process I review a series of films and how they communicate these worldviews. I complete the section with a cursory examination of some other worldviews that are also present in modern films, such as fate, monism, emergent evolution and neopagan-ism (chapter five).

In the third and last part, "Spirituality in the Movies," I examine how different elements of Christianity have been dealt with in films. First, I look at how Christians and their faith have been portrayed in both a good and a bad light in recent years (chapter six). Then I address how movies have dealt with angels, demons, heaven and hell (chapter seven). Last, I investigate how movies deal with the nature of faith through three dominant motifs: blind faith versus proof, individual faith versus organized religion, and doubt versus faith (chapter eight).

In the conclusion I make some suggestions for the reader on how to encourage dialogue when discussing movies, how to avoid the extreme reactions of cultural anorexia and gluttony, and how to deal with the biblical issue of the "weaker brother" and moviegoing.

Throughout the text, the reader will find what I have titled "Director's Cuts." These point the reader to online essays and fragments complementary to this book, along with other free articles available on the Internet and books that discuss the topic at hand in more detail. At the end of each chapter I have added some "Watch and Learn" suggestions for watching movies and applying the lessons learned in that chapter. Practical action steps will help develop and sharpen discernment skills.

Fair Warning

The reader should be aware that on the following pages I reveal important plot twists and character revelations about specific movies. Regrettably, this is unavoidable because much of the worldview and philosophy of a film is wrapped up in these twists. But be encouraged—good stories are often not hindered by such foreknowledge. If you demand total innocence regarding the plots of movies you intend to see, then skip over discussions of those movies as you encounter them in the text.

Well, here it is: Movie Appreciation 101. What follows are the confessions of a screenwriter: how we storytellers try to influence you, the audience, with our worldviews.

*   *   *

Are You a Cultural Glutton or a Cultural Anorexic?

Ask yourself these questions to challenge your personal growth.

Cultural Glutton

1. Do you watch every movie that interests you without considering beforehand whether its subject matter is appropriate?

2. Do you think movies and television are only entertainment without any real messages?

3. How many hours a week do you spend on entertainment? Now compare that with how many hours a week you read the Bible or other spiritual growth material.

4. How many times have you enjoyed a movie that you later came to realize was offensive to your beliefs or worldview?

Cultural Anorexic

1. Do you generalize all movies as "worldly" or consider any depiction of sin as wrong without concern for context?

2. Are you unable to appreciate anything good in a movie because of some bad you see in it?

3. Do you consider art and entertainment to be wastes of time and therefore spend all of your leisure time on "spiritual" activities?

4. How many times have you been incapable of interacting with those around you because you were out of touch with their cultural experience?

Part 1

Storytelling
in the Movies

 Stories
& Mythology

Every story is informed by a worldview. And so every movie, being a dramatic story, is also informed by a worldview. There is no such thing as a neutral story in which events and characters are presented objectively apart from interpretation. Every choice an author makes, from what kinds of characters she creates to which events she includes, is determined by the author's worldview. A worldview even defines what a character or event *is* for the writer—and therefore for the audience. And the worldview or philosophy of a film is conveyed much in the same way as stories of old would convey the values and beliefs of ancient societies—through dramatic incarnation of those values. In a sense, movies are the new myths of American culture.

Christopher Vogler, accomplished educator of writers and student of famous mythologist Joseph Campbell, explains the nature of myth:

What is a myth? For our purposes a myth is not the untruth or fanciful exaggeration of popular expression. A myth, as Joseph Campbell was fond of saying, is a metaphor for a mystery beyond human comprehension. It is a comparison that helps us understand, by analogy, some aspect of our mysterious selves. A myth, in this way of thinking, is not an untruth but a way of reaching a profound truth.

Then what is a story? A story is also a metaphor, *a model of some aspect of human behavior.*[1]

In the PBS series *The Power of Myth* we get the nod from Campbell himself about just what story does for us:

BILL MOYERS: So we tell stories to try to come to terms with the world, to harmonize ourselves with reality?

JOSEPH CAMPBELL: I think so, yes.[2]

Famous psychoanalyst Bruno Bettelheim agrees. Writing in *The Uses of Enchantment* (his classic on the meaning and importance of fairy tales), he says, "Myths and fairy stories both answer the eternal questions: What is the world really like? How am I to live my life in it? How can I truly be myself?"[3]

Since the beginning of time, humankind has used story to convey the meaning and purpose of life. Within its various forms (myth, fable, parable, allegory), and within its development from oral tradition to codification, storytelling has through the eons been the backbone of civilizations. It has maintained ritual, systematized beliefs and taught dogma. In essence, story incarnates the myths and values of a culture with the intent of perpetuating them. Moses' Pentateuch tells the story of the redemption of the Hebrews. The Babylonian *Epic of Gilgamesh* tells the heroic redemption of its principal character, Gilgamesh. Homer's epic poem *The*

---

[1]Christopher Vogler, *The Writer's Journey* (Studio City, Calif.: Michael Wiese Productions, 1992), p. vii. The emphasis is mine.

[2]Joseph Campbell with Bill Moyers, *The Power of Myth* (New York: Doubleday, 1988), p. 4.

[3]Bruno Bettelheim, *The Uses of Enchantment: The Meaning and Importance of Fairy Tales* (New York: Random House, 1989), p. 45. Unfortunately, Bettelheim's analysis of fairy tales suffers the excesses of a myopic Freudianism.

Odyssey is the tale of the redemptive journeys of Odysseus.

We now live in a world permeated with science and technology, but does that make us any less storytellers or any less myth-oriented in our lives? Our culture still thrives on storytelling in many manifestations, including news, books, music and movies, to name a few. The very nature of moviemaking and moviegoing itself incarnates the sacred transmission of myth, much as occurred for the ancients. As author Geoffrey Hill proposes in his treatise on the mythic power of film, *Illuminating Shadows:*

> As ironic modern worshippers we congregate at the cinematic temple. We pay our votive offerings at the box office. We buy our ritual corn. We hush in reverent anticipation as the lights go down and the celluloid magic begins. Throughout the filmic narrative we identify with the hero. We vilify the antihero. We vicariously exult in the victories of the drama. And we are spiritually inspired by the moral of the story, all while believing we are modern techno-secular people, devoid of religion. Yet the depth and intensity of our participation reveal a religious fervor that is not much different from that of religious zealots.[4]

While the interpretation of *all* moviegoing as religious liturgy may be strained, it is certainly a caution to the viewer to avoid an identification with the cultural glutton who, through lack of discernment, often falls prey to such manipulation. Perhaps Hill's thesis of the transference of sacred storytelling of the past into the secular moviegoing of the present would better serve the argument that no story exists neutrally as raw entertainment without reference to cultural beliefs and values. Neglecting the importance of the worldview behind a movie amounts to a denial of our primal nature as storytellers. It denies as well the influence our stories have on the human psyche, collective *and* individual.

An example of mythological adaptation in our secular society can be found in comic book heroes. Speaking as long ago as 1963, famous anthropologist Mircea Eliade stated, "The characters of comic strips present the

---

[4]Geoffrey Hill, *Illuminating Shadows: The Mythic Power of Film* (Boston: Shambhala, 1992), p. 3.

modern version of mythological or folklore Heros."[5] The proliferation of comic books being adapted into movies signals a contemporary hunger for hero worship, the desire for redemption through the salvific acts of deity. Witness *Superman I-IV* (1978-1987), *Batman I-IV* (1989-1997), *Dick Tracy* (1990), *Teenage Mutant Ninja Turtles I-III* (1990-1993), *The Shadow* (1994), *Judge Dredd* (1995), *Barb Wire* (1996), *The Phantom* (1996), *Spawn* (1997), *Steel* (1997), *Blade* (1998), *Mystery Men* (1999), *X-Men* (2000) and *Spider-Man* (2002). And that's not even mentioning all the television adaptations, from *Wonder Woman* (1974) and *Smallville* (2001) to the myriad of children's cartoon versions of many more comic book series. Witness also the many comic book hero movies currently in development at various studios as I write this book, including *The Green Lantern, The Fantastic Four, The Incredible Hulk, Catwoman, The Silver Surfer, Sub-Mariner, Daredevil, Captain America* and *Ghost Rider.*

In all these comic book-based stories there is a projection of super powers onto individuals much in the same way that the gods were projections of pagan hope. Watching *X-Men,* for instance, with all its superheroes and supervillains in our contemporary world, brings to mind the pantheon of Greek gods from Mount Olympus battling it out over mortal human beings. Each god in the pantheon had a special power: Hermes, the messenger of the gods, could run with fleet-winged feet; Hephaestus was the god of fire. Likewise, each of the mutant X-Men has a power that enables him or her to battle evil or do evil: Mystique can change her shape to appear to be something else; Storm can call forth the powers of nature; Magneto has powers of magnetism. The spiritual aspect of these abilities has been secularized, reinterpreted through evolutionary myth as the result of mutation, but the metaphor remains the same. As Francis Schaeffer has pointed out, the gods of Greece and Rome were actually "amplified humanity, not divinity."[6]

The story of Superman is a classic American tale that many say

---

[5]Mircea Eliade, *Myth and Reality* (New York: Harper & Row, 1963), pp. 184-85.
[6]Francis Schaeffer, *How Should We Then Live?* (Westchester, Ill.: Crossway, 1982), p. 85.

embodies a mythical retelling of the life of Christ. Whether or not this is true, Eliade opines of Superman's preternatural identity hidden behind his Clark Kent humanity, "This humiliating camouflage of a Hero whose powers are literally unlimited revives a well-known mythical theme. In the last analysis, the myth of Superman satisfies the secret longings of modern man who, though he knows that he is a fallen, limited creature, dreams of one day proving himself an 'exceptional person,' a 'Hero.' "[7]

Another popular source of American mythology is the western genre. Values like rugged individualism, the pioneer spirit, vigilante justice, outlaws as heroes, restlessness of spirit and love of outdoors run deep in many Americans' hearts and in many American westerns.

A typical western movie reinforces the image of the lone, righteous man facing a savage world, carving his way through a harsh, rugged terrain, burly outlaws and wild Indians in order for civilization to find its roots. With a six-gun on his hip and a warrior code of honor, the cowboy hands out posse justice to outlaws who endanger the growth of the village. Morality is a law of the jungle, solved by survival of the fittest.

The antiwestern is an overturning of the mythology of the western by showing the dark side of the aforesaid values. Movies like *Unforgiven* (1992), *Wyatt Earp* (1994) and *Ravenous* (1999) are antiwesterns that show the values of the American West to have been founded on questionable or even immoral premises.

In David Webb Peoples's Oscar-winning *Unforgiven,* the characters struggle with the reality of killing people and the romantic hype that surrounds unrealistic heroes and villains through dime-store fiction novels. It shows that shooting men dead is not as easy and without spiritual consequences as most westerns would make us believe. Ironically, its star, Clint Eastwood, is himself one of the spaghetti western icons whom this movie deconstructs. In the end, the "hero" must become villainous himself in order to defeat the villains, blurring the line between the white hats and the black hats, between good guys and bad guys.

---

[7]Eliade, *Myth and Reality,* p. 185.

Ravenous, written by Ted Griffin, is the story of a cannibal terrorizing a California outpost during the Mexican-American War, just before the Gold Rush. American westward expansion is symbolized as a cannibalizing of the environment and native cultures with the notion of American Manifest Destiny—the popular doctrine that the United States had the right and duty to expand throughout the North American continent. *Ravenous* is a turning of the tables on the western myth by proverbializing it as cannibalism.

Mythology is far from dead even in a modern technological and secularized world. And movies are one of the most effective means of communicating mythology because they are a story-centered medium that captures and reflects our deeply held beliefs.

Mythology, Paganism and Christianity

Joseph Campbell has become a saint to many in Hollywood, thanks to the evangelistic efforts of such apostles as George Lucas and Christopher Vogler. Campbell's approach to mythology is akin to Jung's concept of the archetypes residing in the individual and collective unconscious.

Like Carl Jung, Campbell believed that the individual unconscious mind of each person is an extension of the unified "collective unconscious"—an amalgamation of all of humankind's ancestral experience. Our minds share in the pool of all human psyche throughout the ages, like many individuals sharing in the same dream. His monism concludes, "The essence of oneself and the essence of the world: These two are one."[8]

According to Campbell, all religions and mythologies are but local manifestations of the single truth of what he calls the "Monomyth" of the hero. The Monomyth, in its most basic form, consists of the hero's journey from separation to initiation to return,[9] and it embodies redemption in a way we will discuss in the next chapter on story structure. Campbell attempts to prove his thesis with an eclectic recitation of many of the

---

[8]Joseph Campbell, *The Hero with a Thousand Faces* (Princeton, N.J.: Princeton University Press, 1973), p. 386.
[9]Ibid., p. 30.

world's stories, from their creation myths to their flood legends and
heroes of faith.

Vogler puts it simply: "All stories consist of a few common structural
elements found universally in myths, fairy tales, dreams, and movies.
They are known collectively as The Hero's Journey."[10] It is difficult to
deny this common thread among diverse cultures, and the Christian need
not fear facing such facts. After all, the meaning of so-called facts is in
the interpretation, and the interpretation is in the worldview.[11] So how
does the Christian deal with such mythical similarities among cultures?

Christians need not deny a Monomyth that is reinterpreted through
different traditions. We need only understand
it in its true nature from God's own revelation.
After all, God is the ultimate Storyteller, and
the Scriptures say that he has placed a common knowledge of himself in all people
through creation and conscience (Romans
1:18-20; 2:15). This explains the true genesis
and nature of the Monomyth. In running from
God, heathen humanity distorts that Monomyth of knowledge inside themselves. Thus all
religions and rituals have the scent of an original truth that has been turned into the stench of a lie:

 **Director's Cut**

SCP Journal **devoted an
entire issue to examining
Joseph Campbell and his
theories; see** *SCP Journal*
**9, no. 2 (1990). Visit
‹www.godawa.com› for
critiques of Joseph
Campbell's ideology.**

> Even though [human beings] knew God, they did not honor Him as God,
> or give thanks; but they became futile in their speculations, and their fool-
> ish heart was darkened. Professing to be wise, they became fools, and
> exchanged the glory of the incorruptible God for an image in the form of
> corruptible man and of birds and four-footed animals and crawling crea-
> tures. . . . They exchanged the truth of God for a lie, and worshiped and
> served the creature rather than the Creator, who is blessed forever. Amen.
> (Romans 1:21-23, 25)

---

[10]Vogler, *Writer's Journey*, p. 3.
[11]Campbell's individual interpretation is founded on relativistic monism, which does not comport with Christianity.

It should not surprise us or scare us that all cultures have creation myths, flood legends and similar ritualistic concepts. We should expect it. And we should not tremble at modern scholarship that sees historical fabrication in mythical origins. Just because there is similarity in myth between Christianity and other religions does not mean that Christianity is on an equal playing field with these religions or subordinate to a more generic Monomyth. Christianity is itself the true incarnation of the Monomyth in history, and other mythologies reflect and distort it like dirty or broken mirrors.

In addition to providing this true underlying mythology of reality, Christianity alone provides the justification for storytelling. Robert W. Jenson, in an article explaining "how the world has lost its story," points out that the very precondition for the intelligibility of storytelling is itself a "narratable world."[12] That is, the biblical notion of linear history, with an author, characters and a purposeful goal, was the philosophical foundation for the search for meaning in a narrative of life. Storytelling is meaningless gibberish unless reality itself is narratable.

Author Daniel Taylor comments on this legacy of Western culture's biblical heritage of living in a narratable world. In order to tell a story with plot and characters that are not in utter chaos, one must already believe that reality is explainable, he says, and "that belief depends on a number of supporting beliefs: that reality is at least in part knowable; that there are meaningful connections between events; that actions have consequences; that humans do most things by choice, not by irresistible compulsion; that we are therefore responsible; and so on."[13]

We are creatures of story, created by a storytelling God, who created the very fabric of our reality in terms of his story. Rather than seeing our existence as a series of unconnected random events without purpose, storytelling brings meaning to our lives through the analogy of carefully crafted plot that reflects the loving sovereignty of the God of the Bible.

---

[12]Robert W. Jenson, "How the World Lost Its Story," *First Things* 36 (October 1993): 19-24.
[13]Daniel Taylor, *The Healing Power of Stories: Creating Yourself Through the Stories of Your Life* (Dublin: Gill & Macmillan, 1996), p. 140.

As Taylor concludes:

> Stories link past, present and future in a way that tells us where we have been (even before we were born), where we are, and where we could be going. . . . Our stories teach us that there is a place for us, that we fit. They suggest to us that our lives can have a plot. Stories turn mere chronology, one thing after another, into the purposeful action of plot, and thereby into meaning. . . . Stories are the single best way humans have for accounting for our experience.[14]

God is such a creative author that he embodies both myth *and* history into his own narrative of redemption. As C. S. Lewis put it:

> The heart of Christianity is a myth which is also a fact. . . . By becoming fact, it does not cease to be myth: That is the miracle. I suspect that men have sometimes derived more spiritual sustenance from myths they did not believe than from the religion they professed. To be truly Christian we must both assent to the historical fact and also receive the myth (fact though it has become) with the same imaginative embrace which we accord to all myths. The one is hardly more necessary than the other. . . . We must not be ashamed of the mythical radiance resting on our theology. We must not be nervous about "parallels" and "Pagan Christs": they ought to be there—it would be a stumbling block if they weren't. We must not, in false spirituality, withhold our imaginative welcome.[15]

J. R. R. Tolkien was the master storyteller who led C. S. Lewis to Christ with this kind of myth-become-fact reasoning. In Tolkien's famous lecture "On Fairy-Stories" he speaks of approaching the "Christian story" with joy because the nature of fantasy and even happy endings (which he calls "eucatastrophe") gives us a "sudden glimpse of the underlying reality or truth" of the ultimate happy ending: the resurrection of Christ and the believer's sharing in that resurrection.

---

[14]Ibid., pp. 1-2.
[15]C. S. Lewis, *God in the Dock: Essays on Theology and Ethics,* ed. Walter Hooper (Grand Rapids, Mich.: Eerdmans, 1970), pp. 66-67.

The Gospels contain a fairy-story, or a story of a larger kind which embraces all the essence of fairy-stories. They contain marvels—peculiarly artistic, beautiful and moving: "mythical" in their perfect, self-contained significance; and among the marvels is the greatest and most complete conceivable eucatastrophe. But this story has entered History and the primary world; the desire and aspiration of sub-creation has been raised to the fulfillment of Creation. The Birth of Christ is the eucatastrophe of Man's history. The Resurrection is the eucatastrophe of the story of the Incarnation. This story begins and ends in joy. It has pre-eminently the "inner consistency of reality". There is no tale ever told that men would rather find was true, and none which so many sceptical men have accepted as true on its own merits. For the Art of it has the supremely convincing tone of Primary Art, that is, of Creation. To reject it leads either to sadness or to wrath.[16]

Christ Mythology

Christianity has a mythology of its own, one that embodies the common elements of the hero's journey but brings with it unique concepts like substitutionary atonement and unmerited grace. An example of this has already been pointed out above in the myth of Superman. Let's take a look at how some other modern movies have embodied the Christ mythology into their stories, thereby reinforcing or deconstructing its influence.

A positive Christ myth is resurrected in *The Green Mile* (1999), adapted by Frank Darabont from the novel by Stephen King. This movie rewraps the Christ story into a racial context by incarnating the Christ figure in a huge, wrongly accused black man, condemned to die in the electric chair for murdering two small girls in the rural South of the 1930s.

The prison guards soon learn that the prisoner, John Coffey (whose initials are the same as Jesus Christ's), is able to heal people's infirmities

---

[16]J. R. R. Tolkien, "On Fairy-Stories," in *The Monsters and the Critics and Other Essays,* ed. Christopher Tolkien (London: George Allen & Unwin, 1983), pp. 155-56.

by touching the affected parts of their bodies. At first Coffey resurrects a dead mouse, then he heals the head guard (played by Tom Hanks) of a urinary tract infection, and finally he heals the warden's wife of a deathbed tumor. During the healings, we see Coffey take the disease onto himself and then spit it out in the form of a swarm of flies. In the Bible, Satan is given the name Beelzebub, which means "Lord of the Flies," so healing represents a redemption from his power.

John Coffey ends up dying for the crimes of the real killer, the innocent in place of the guilty. He is led like a lamb to the slaughter at his execution, and death is swallowed up in victory as the electric chair is never used again—and the resurrected mouse lives on forever. *The Green Mile* retells the story of Christ as a "pure soul" who is punished by the world.

Other movies, like *Being There* (1979), *E.T.* (1982), *Jesus of Montreal* (1989), *Powder* (1995), *Phenomenon* (1996), *Spitfire Grill* (1996), *Sling Blade* (1996) and *The Mask of Zorro* (1998), use the Christ myth as a paradigm for their lead characters—unlikely, hesitant heroes who are rejected by their society but are in the end embraced as saviors. Screenwriter Randall Wallace has expressed his intent behind *Braveheart* (1995) as its being a reflection of the gospel. In the same way that William Wallace's martyrdom became the loss that won Scotland's freedom, so our own spiritual freedom is wrought from the self-sacrifice of Jesus Christ.

The Matrix (1999), the sci-fi phenomenon written and directed by the Wachowski brothers, is a mixing of Greek and Christian mythology similar to the Neo-Platonism of earlier centuries. The parallels are obvious: Neo ("new man," "new Adam," played by Keanu Reeves) is "the Chosen One" (Christ) who is prophesied to come and free the people from the deadly, controlling matrix that has enslaved all humans from birth, similar to the blind slavery of sin that everyone born into Adam has inherited (Romans 5). When people are awakened (enlightened) from their bondage, they appear like newborn babies from their life support pods, seeing the universal bondage all around them with new eyes, much like spiritual rebirth for the Christian (John 3).

Neo delivers an illegal computer disk to a fellow hacker, who jokingly says of Neo, "Hallelujah. You're my savior. My own personal Jesus Christ." When people are freed from the delusion of the matrix, they go to a city called Zion—the same name as the biblical city of the Promised Land that is fulfilled in the church as the body of Christ.

Laurence Fishburne plays Morpheus (the name of the Greek god of the dead), who doubles as John the Baptist heralding the coming of the chosen one, a voice crying in the wilderness. And Morpheus is captain of the hovercraft Nebuchadnezzar, named after the Babylonian king in the Bible whose dreams only Daniel could interpret. Trinity is the name of Carrie-Anne Moss's character.

Neo is betrayed by Cypher, a Judas of the good-guy disciples. The messianic implications are crystallized when Neo gives his life to save Morpheus. He dies but comes back to life, resurrected by the kiss (breath) of Trinity, only to miraculously defeat the enemy. In the last shot of the movie Neo ascends into heaven in the clouds as he heralds his followers on a new quest to preach their gospel to all creation, that is, to all those in bondage to the matrix.

Hannibal (2001), the sequel to the Academy Award-winning *Silence of the Lambs,* written by David Mamet and Steven Zaillian, is an anti-Christ myth, that is, a retelling of the Christ story turned upside down by giving the villain, the infamous Hannibal Lecter, the Christ role. Pazzi, the Italian cop who tracks down Hannibal in Florence, is a clear Judas rewrite. Not only does he betray Hannibal for $3 million (a multiple of the thirty pieces of Judas's silver), but also he is killed in exactly the same way as Judas, by hanging and having his bowels spill out. And all this after a history lesson about the biblical Judas Iscariot given by Hannibal himself.

Director's Cut

For further reading about Jesus and Christ mythology in the movies, see the online essay "Jesus in the Movies" at ‹www.godawa.com›.

Hannibal has a gruesome "last supper" with Clarice (his nemesis *and* love interest) that is quite literally the eating of a body. When he discov-

The Matrix	Christianity	Greek Religion
Morpheus: Declares "the One"	John the Baptist: Proclaims the Christ	Morpheus: God of dreams
Morpheus: A father to them	Father	
Neo	Son ("New Adam")	Greek for "new man"/ anagram of "one"
Trinity	Holy Spirit	Goddess
Slaves to A.I.	Slaves to sin	Plato's cave
Wake up in pod	Spiritual rebirth	Enlightenment
Cypher	Judas	
Oracle	Prophet	Oracle of Delphi ("Know thyself")
The One	Christ	Plato's philosopher king
Neo resurrected	Jesus resurrected	
Neo flies away	Jesus ascended into heaven	
Return of the One	The second coming	
Zion: The last human city	Zion: Promised Land/ body of Christ	
Nebuchadnezzar: Hovercraft	Nebuchadnezzar: King of Babylon (had dreams)	

Figure 1. Christian and Greek parallels in *The Matrix*

ers Clarice's self-loathing thoughts, he jabs that she would like the apostle Paul because he hated women too. (In other words, Paul taught biblical patriarchy: women are to be subject to their husbands as their husbands are subject to Christ.)

Finally Hannibal escapes, "ascending to heaven" in a jumbo jet. *Hannibal* ends up an ironic postmodern recasting of the Christ story—in a way, a fitting expression of our social decay and cultural depravity.

Demythologization

One modern mythology is the naturalistic worldview. In this view primitive peoples create myths and religious symbols for natural phenomena they do not understand. Since naturalists believe there are no true spiritual realities, only natural phenomena, they assume that there must be a natural explanation behind every myth or religious belief. For instance, if a culture does not understand thunder, it reinterprets thunder to represent a deity in order to make sense of it. The goal of the naturalist, then, is to discover what natural experiences cultures had that drove them to create such mythology.

Movies like *Stargate* (1997), *A.I.* (2001), *Cast Away* (2001) and *Planet of the Apes* (2001) are strong examples of this demythologizing tendency. In chapter five *A.I.* is discussed in detail within the context of evolution, and *Cast Away* is discussed within the context of fate. So let's take a look at *Planet of the Apes*. In this so-called reimagining of the original story by Pierre Boulle, screenwriter William Broyles Jr. tells the story of a young American space scientist, Captain Leo Davidson (played by Mark Wahlberg), who works with genetically enhanced monkeys on a ship in deep space. His favorite experimental chimp pilots a test vehicle and is lost in a strange space storm. Leo goes after his simian buddy and is lost in a time-warping wormhole that lands him on a planet ruled by talking apes who enslave and abuse humans. The story is a predictable action-genre pursuit of the hero, who is trying to escape so that he can go home to his mother ship.

It turns out that these apes pray to a "god," Semos, who "created all apes in his image" and who came from the skies, landed in the "the Forbidden Zone," which is called "Calima," and ascended into the heavens, from whence he promised to return. The parallels with Genesis, Eden and the return of Christ are obvious. Leo makes his way to that forbidden area because he gets a radio signal that leads him to believe his mother ship is somewhere near there. And right he is, because the Forbidden Zone contains Leo's original spaceship, which had crash-landed on the planet while trying to find Leo. The twist is that the mother ship had gone through the time warp as well and had landed on the planet many years before Leo arrived. So the apes are descendants, with modification, from the original genetically enhanced monkeys aboard Leo's own ship, and the humans are descendants of the original crew. Semos is the name of one of those original monkeys. Another naturalistic spin is that the title of "Calima," as the Edenic origin, came from a misreading of a dirt-obstructed plaque with the title "Caution Live Animals" (shades of V'ger in *Star Trek: The Movie:* important beliefs are often linguistic misreadings).

At the end of the movie, after a big battle between apes and humans, the original spaceship that Leo was trying to find comes out of the wormhole and lands in the middle of the masses of slack-jawed apes and humans. The chimp inside is like an ancient astronaut in a chariot of the gods. The apes of course think this chimp is Semos and bow in religious worship like it is the return of Christ. Leo knows better and goes to hug his pet, winning the day. The demythology is clear: the true natural origins of the apes on the planet got distorted and obscured through eons of time and ignorance into religious myths, in order for the apes to explain to themselves what they could not understand. The analogy is that humankind has done the same thing in creating religions.

While there may be some truth to the natural origins of some religious beliefs, demythology, as an absolute interpretation of history, suffers from its own mythological bias. The writer of *Gladiator* (2000), David Franzoni, explained that he was working on a King Arthur script "which aims more for history than myth."[17] What Franzoni does not mention is that there is no certifiable history of King Arthur. All we have are medieval romances, Welsh legends and other academic speculations of his exploits. To say that one will "aim more for history than

> **Director's Cut**
>
> For further reading that critiques the nature of demythology and higher criticism of the Bible, see Gleason L. Archer, *A Survey of Old Testament Introduction* (Chicago: Moody Press, 1996). Also visit my website: ‹www.godawa.com›.

---

[17]John Soriano, "WGA.org's Exclusive Interview with David Franzoni," WGA <www.wga.org/craft/interviews/franzoni2001.html>.

myth" is really to say that one will aim more for one myth or legend over other myths and legends. The art of demythologizing is itself a mythology that believes there are no preternatural or transcendent mysteries to life, so it interprets what it cannot understand or does not know in terms of its own naturalistic cause-and-effect bias. This is not to say that all myth and history are equal in factual value, but it is a strong challenge to those who neglect to understand that even historical accounts are filtered through the historian's bias.

Myth and Meaning

From the Greek tragedies of Euripides to the bawdy comedies of Shakespeare, both ancient and classical writers suffered no shame in telling a good story with the intention of proving a point or illustrating how they believed we ought to live in this world. Storytelling from its inception was expected to be more than entertainment.

Through their craft, the first storytellers were expected to teach the culture how to live and behave in their world. The rejection of "messages" in movies as "preachy" or "propaganda" is a recent phenomenon that results from the splitting of reality into secular/sacred distinctions, as if a story about human beings relating to one another could exist in a vacuum, without reference to values or meaning.

Joseph Campbell was worried about the thoughtless irresponsibility of modern movie narrative. He called our storytellers to return to one of the primary functions of myth: its pedagogical nature, teaching how to live a human life under any circumstances.[18] This return to the craft as high priesthood is a recognition of the privilege and responsibility that storytellers have in "making and breaking lives" by the power of their medium and its message.[19]

True, some movies are more obvious or blatant than others in their message, and some are simpler or less focused than others, but all of

---

[18]Campbell, *Hero*, p. 31.
[19]Ibid., p. 8.

them communicate values and worldviews nonetheless. This is a matter of degree, not of essence. Often the very movies that people think are not meaningful are actually loaded with powerful messages and worldviews.

For example, the gross-out comedy *There's Something About Mary* (1998) is, as explained by its writers, (the Farrelly brothers), all about the nature of true love. As we embark on the pursuit by the hero, Ted (played by Ben Stiller), to reconnect with his high school love interest, Mary (played by Cameron Diaz), the only woman he ever truly cared for, we find that his infatuation is no less selfish than that of the various other stalkers obsessed with the same woman. Only when he realizes this and decides to make Mary happy by finding her the man of her dreams, rather than focusing on her being the woman of *his* dreams, does Ted achieve the character and integrity necessary to be the right person to love. The movie's message is that true love is the willingness to give up one's own happiness for the happiness of the one you love. *There's Something About Mary* is a profoundly meaningful gross-out comedy.

Rather than spurning mythology as something that only so-called primitive societies have, we ought to recognize that the heart of movie storytelling (modern mythology) is the communication and reinforcement of worldviews and values. And so we ought to judge movies in this light, even getting involved ourselves in creating and telling stories that express redemption for a lost world.

Watch and Learn

1. With a friend or two, watch the movie *Cast Away* (2000). Look for and discuss the symbolic references to the development of humankind in the experience of Chuck on the island. Look also for Chuck's ultimate reconnection with civilization. What do the symbols of the volleyball, time, the angel wings and the whale represent? Discuss the kind of character that Chuck is at the beginning and then how he has changed after his journey. Imagine yourself in his shoes and discuss what aspects of your life you would change if you had the same experience. Discuss what

you think the movie was saying about what is really valuable in life.

2. Watch the movie *Spitfire Grill* with some friends and discuss the elements of the Christ story that you see in the movie.

3. Consider a comedy movie that you never thought was meaningful beyond a bunch of jokes and gags. Now rewatch that movie and discuss the journey of the main character. What was he or she like at the beginning of the movie? What did this person learn or not learn? How did the character change, or how did the character change others, by the end of the movie? If you were to see the movie as a parable, what would be its main message?

② Redemption

Two of the most frustrating replies to hear when asking people what they thought of a movie are "I liked it" or "I didn't like it," *accompanied by an inability to explain why.* But with an elementary understanding of the structure of storytelling, an informed moviegoer can watch a film and enjoy the story while also engaging his or her critical faculties to understand what the movie is trying to say about the way in which we ought or ought not to live.

We have already established that stories do not exist in a vacuum of meaninglessness. Movies communicate prevailing myths and cultural values. And this cultural effect is far deeper than the excesses of sex and violence. It extends to the philosophy behind the film. The way we view the world and things like right and wrong are embodied in the redemptive structure of storytelling itself.

It is not necessary that audiences are even consciously aware that a message or worldview is being communicated. The composition of a story leads a viewer through emotional and dramatic experiences to see things in the way the storytellers want the viewer to see. This is similar to the visual form, color and composition used by a painter to guide a viewer's eyes and mind to see what the painter wants him to see.

Now let's take a look at these structural elements, with movies to illustrate each one.[1] We will examine two films that are similar in theme but opposite in their worldview as well as being opposite in genre: *Amadeus,* the 1984 Oscar-winning tragedy about the man who killed Mozart (in the movie, though not in reality); and *The Truman Show,* the 1998 Jim Carrey comedy vehicle about an innocent and naive young man who discovers that his life is a TV show for the world.

Theme

The first element to consider when analyzing a movie is its theme. Every good movie has a theme. Some may call it "the moral of the story"; others may call it "the message"; but the theme is what the story is ultimately all about. You can state a theme propositionally as a premise that leads to a conclusion. It can usually be stated in terms of "x leads to y"[2] or some other prescriptive equivalent, such as "Fear of differences in others leads to alienation" *(Shrek)* or "Greed leads to self-destruction" *(Indecent Proposal* and *A Simple Plan).*

Other examples of themes include the following. *Traffic:* In the war on drugs, no one gets away clean, not even the good guys. *Babe:* Biology can be transcended by personal choice (a pig proves that he *can* be a sheepdog). *Fatal Attraction:* Infidelity turns against itself. *Dead Poets Society:* Conformity kills the spirit, but individuality frees it. *Terminator*

---

[1]A dominant influence on my summary of storytelling structure in this chapter is John Truby's lectures called "Great Screenwriting Class." And the source for much of Truby's teaching was Joseph Campbell's insights into the heroic Monomyth. Campbell, of course, was simply drawing from the commonality of all world religions (which, as discussed in chapter one, are merely distortions of the true Christian Monomyth). John Truby's "Great Screenwriting Class" tapes, as well as other helpful tapes on genres, can be purchased at <http://hollywoodnet.com/Truby/univ.html>.

[2]Lajos Egri, *The Art of Dramatic Writing: Its Basis in the Creative Interpretation of Human Motives* (New York: Simon & Schuster, 1960), pp. 1-32.

and *Jurassic Park:* Unfettered technology turns against humanity.

The theme is the purpose or moral of the story, and it is incarnate in the plot. Aristotle described plot as the inevitable or probable sequence of events.[3] If we claim that a sequence of events is inevitable from a character's beginning behavior, then we are making a moral claim about the world. X leads to y. If we behave in such a way, such an end will result. Our story fleshes out our theme.

Amadeus, written by Peter Shaffer, is the story of Antonio Salieri, the court composer of Austrian Emperor Joseph II. Salieri is a man who from an early age desired to glorify God by composing great music. But he soon realizes that God has instead chosen the childish infidel Wolfgang Amadeus Mozart for divine creativity. Salieri is so angered at God's seeming capriciousness that he eventually decides to get revenge on God by destroying Mozart. His attempts land him in an insane asylum. The theme: True freedom is found in accepting one's fate or destiny from God; trying to control one's destiny leads to slavery.

The Truman Show, written by Andrew Niccol, is about a naive young man named Truman, who dreams of leaving his small, idyllic town of Seahaven to see the world and find his true love. Every attempt he makes to leave is blocked until he discovers that his entire life has been a TV show controlled by a godlike television producer named Christof. Truman must confront his inner demons as well as the producer of the show to free himself from external controls and choose his own destiny in life. The theme of *The Truman Show* is that true freedom is found in controlling one's own destiny. God's sovereign control of our lives leads to slavery; human autonomy leads to freedom.

As you can see, both stories—*Amadeus* and *The Truman Show*—deal with the theme of God's sovereignty and human freedom, yet they arrive at opposite conclusions.

Many movies contain several themes. Some may be more general than others. For example, an additional theme of *The Truman Show* is the notion that media in America have become an all-consuming substitute

---

[3]Aristotle, *Aristotle's Poetics,* trans. James Hutton (New York: W. W. Norton, 1982), p. 53.

for living real life. But even this theme serves the bigger theme of life as autonomous freedom.

The Hero

With theme established, let's look at the basic structure of the story. Most moviegoers are familiar with the idea that stories have heroes and villains. Simply put, the hero is the main character, the one whom the story is about. The hero of *The Truman Show* is obviously Truman. *Amadeus* has a unique take on the hero because, in a sense, the villain is the hero. Salieri is the one trying to fight God and kill Mozart, and these facts make him the villain. But Peter Shaffer turns the perspective around and shows us the story through the villain's eyes as if he were the hero. So, to Salieri, God is the villain.

The Hero's Goal

The hero always has a goal, a strong desire that drives the story. Without a goal, there is no story. And the hero is usually driven to the point of obsession with this goal.

For Salieri, his goal begins as a desire to glorify God with beautiful and famous music. From his youth, he sets out to achieve that goal by studying music with all his heart.

Truman's goal is to leave the small town he was brought up in and go to a distant, exotic location like Fiji. But Truman also has a secondary goal of finding the girl with whom he fell in love in an earlier time of his life.

The Adversary

The adversary is the external opponent of the hero and the hero's goal. I use the word *adversary* rather than *villain* because the word *villain* often conjures up the stereotype of Snidely Whiplash versus Dudley Do-Right, and this viewpoint can miss the finer distinctions and subtleties of more complex characters.[4] In essence, the adversary represents the contrasting

---

[4]Writers often call the hero "protagonist" and the villain "antagonist" for the same reason of avoiding extremes and stereotypes.

belief system to that of the hero, resulting in a story that is ultimately a clash of worldviews. An adversary may be an individual, like Scar in *The Lion King,* or a force, like chance in *Forrest Gump,* or nature, as in *The Perfect Storm.* An adversary can be black-and-white evil, like a James Bond nemesis, or a complex character with positive virtues, like Sally Field's character in *Mrs. Doubtfire* or the math professor trying to help the genius Will in *Good Will Hunting.*

The adversary in *The Truman Show* is Christof, who is ultimately a symbol for God. It is no coincidence that his name suggests "Christ-off" and that he speaks to Truman at the end as God might speak, "from the heavens." His desire is for Truman's good, but he ultimately keeps Truman from going to Fiji, which is Truman's goal.

On an earthly level, Salieri's adversary is Mozart, but really Mozart becomes the tangible symbol for God's choice being in opposition to Salieri's desire. Salieri simply cannot accept that God chooses a pagan to produce divine music and relegates a devout believer like himself to the ash heap of mediocrity.

Character Flaw

The hero wants something badly to begin with. That desire is the goal. The adversary blocks the hero from achieving that goal, but an internal opponent also holds him back: the character flaw.

At the beginning of the story, the hero sees life in the wrong way, and by the end of the story, he learns the right way to behave or think within life. This progression of change is what is referred to as the "character arc," the process by which a character changes his paradigm, seeking a *want* but discovering a *need* and responding to that need appropriately or not. If the character learns to respond appropriately, you have a comedy or drama; if the character does not respond appropriately, you have a comedy or tragedy.

In *The Truman Show,* Truman desires to leave his small town and go to Fiji. But his inner flaw is his own innocence and trust of others, which blinds him to the fact that his life is controlled by others, not himself. He also has a fear of water, which is a secondary flaw that keeps him from achieving his goal of leaving Seahaven.

In the beginning of *Amadeus,* Salieri wants to glorify God with great music. But his flaw is that he wants glory out of it for himself. He tries to make a bargain with God on his own terms, vowing that if God will make him famous, he will give God his chastity in return. What he offers is hardly an altruistic exchange, and it's hardly a humble approach to try to bargain with one's Maker.

The Apparent Defeat

The key to the middle of the story is that everything the hero does is blocked by the adversary and the hero's own internal flaw. There is wide latitude here for plot complications and reversals, betrayals and so on. But the important point of the storytelling is to exhaust every possible option that the hero has to achieve his goal, with failure at every turn. There is often a moment of partial victory, like a few wins in a sports season of losses, that gives the hero new hope of achieving the goal. But ultimately every option is played out and the hero cannot achieve what he wants. He may get close, but he cannot get all the way.

Somewhere near the end of this line, the hero faces what is called an "apparent defeat," wherein all the attempts to achieve the goal are frustrated to the point of total futility. Nothing the hero has done works; there are no other options, and the hero is left with no hope of ever achieving his goal.

Then the hero often has a "visit to death" or enters "the gauntlet." "Running the gauntlet" is an old phrase used to describe a form of punishment in which men armed with sticks or other weapons arranged themselves in two lines facing each other and beat the person forced to run between them. The gauntlet can be physical, as it is in *The Truman Show,* where Truman has to battle a sea storm that embodies his worst phobias about water. Or it can be metaphorical, as in *Amadeus,* where Salieri is reading Mozart's compositions and has to "face the music"—Mozart's music, that is—by concluding that he can never achieve this kind of brilliance and beauty and is doomed to a life of mediocrity.

Final Confrontation

The gauntlet usually ends in a final confrontation between the hero and the adversary. This is sometimes called the "obligatory scene" in which the hero and adversary meet face to face and their worldviews come into conflict. It does not always have to be a physical fight; it can be a verbal face-off. The final confrontation is often where the adversary explains his rationale for opposing the hero. Better movies will make this rationale as realistic as possible so as not to create cardboard villains. The adversary's rationale represents the worldview that the writer or storyteller does not want us to accept.

The final confrontation for Truman actually occurs after the sea storm when he hears the godlike voice of Christof from the heavens trying to persuade him not to leave. Their interchange looks and sounds very much like a man quarreling with his Maker, as in Job, only with quite opposite results.

Salieri's final confrontation is his attempt to "write Mozart to death." By pushing Mozart in his sickness, he hopes to drive him to his grave and then perform the very requiem he is transcribing at Mozart's funeral, claiming the authorship for himself! We hear Salieri's rationale throughout the entire film because he is telling us from his "confession" with the priest in the asylum.

Self-Revelation

The hero has a moment in the film, usually near the end, when he learns where he was wrong in what he had desired all along. He realizes that what he *wanted* was not what he *needed*. This is the view that the writer/storyteller is trying to convey to the audience of the way we should or should not live. This moment is the character revelation of the hero, and it represents the theme or moral. It is often closely connected to the final confrontation, either as a result of that confrontation or as the means by which the hero can win the battle.

At the end of *The Truman Show* Truman almost drowns and experiences his own revelation when his boat hits the end of the sky, revealing the dome he has lived in all along. While debating with Christof, he realizes that he must walk away through the little door, into a cold, cruel world. But it is far better to live life free with danger than to live by some other's idea of protection, such as that of a benevolent deity.

In *Amadeus,* Salieri fails to face his self-revelation of God's sovereign control and attempts suicide. After he fails at this as well, he finally goes insane in his willful defiance, calling himself the patron saint of mediocrity and "blessing" the other mental patients around him.

Director's Cut

For further reading on story structure, see Robert McKee, *Story: Substance, Structure, Style and the Principles of Screenwriting* (New York: HarperCollins, 1997); and Michael Hauge, *Writing Screenplays That Sell* (New York: McGraw-Hill, 1991). Lajos Egri examines dramatic writing in the context of thematic purpose in his *The Art of Dramatic Writing: Its Basis in the Creative Interpretation of Human Motives* (New York: Simon & Schuster, 1960). For further reading on storytelling and the movies, visit ‹www.godawa.com›.

Resolution

The resolution (also called the denouément) is a short epilogue to the story showing what results from the hero's change or lack of change. If he has chosen redemption, he has at least begun the restoration of what was lost. He recovers a harmony in his being and life that exemplifies the redemption.

In *The Truman Show* the resolution is left open. In a sense, it doesn't matter how his life ends after his final decision to change, because to the storytellers the point is that it is better to be free with danger and uncertainty ahead than to be protected under the control of deity.

In *Amadeus,* Salieri's insanity is the result of his rejection of redemption, his refusal to submit to God. Because he does not accept his self-revelation, the story is a tragedy, a parable showing us the negative results of a life that defies God. And a life that defies God defies redemption.

Redemption: What It's All About

The reason for walking through these elements of the craft of storytelling used in movies is to illustrate how the essence of storytelling in movies is about redemption. A movie takes a hero with an inner flaw, who desires something and has a plan to get it. But he is blocked by an adversary until he almost fails but finally finds a solution. This process of goal, flaw, failure and self-revelation is the process of paradigm change or conversion in an individual.

A Christian testimony of redemption follows the same structure that a movie does. We, as individuals, have a *goal* for what we want in life to give us significance, fame, money, what have you. But Satan is our *adversary*, and our *character flaw* of sin keeps us from achieving that significance. We think that our control is our salvation, but we are wrong. We are the problem, not the solution. We get to the point in life where our constant attempts at achieving our goal are blocked to the point of *apparent defeat*. We get to the end of ourselves in a *final confrontation* when we realize that either we cannot achieve our misguided worldly goals or else we achieve them and realize that they do not bring the significance we seek. And we finally have a *self-revelation* that what we wanted in life is not what we needed. Our alienation is caused by our own inner faults, our sins. We change our minds (repentance), which results in a changed life, our *resolution*. This is the common personal story of Christian conversion. This is the structure of redemption in stories.

Director's Cut

For a checklist of specific things to look for when watching movies, see "What to Look for in Movies" at ‹www.godawa.com›.

Caveat Emptor: Different Kinds of Redemption

Many films today operate within a humanistic framework of the world. This kind of redemption usually reduces to self-actualization or redemption through self-righteousness. Man is the measure of his own potential. In *Dead Poets Society* the redemption is asserted, by the schoolteacher Keating, that since we are food for the worms and there is no afterlife, we must "seize the day" by casting off social and moral restraint to find one's self or potential.

Story Element	*Amadeus*	*The Truman Show*	**The Apostle Paul's Testimony (Acts 26)**
Theme	Submission to God leads to freedom; personal control leads to slavery.	Submission to God leads to slavery; personal control leads to freedom.	Submission to God leads to freedom; self-righteousness leads to slavery.
Hero	Salieri	Truman	Saul
Goal	To glorify God with famous musical compositions	To leave Seahaven and find the mysterious woman he fell in love with	To attain the hope of the promise made by God to the forefathers by persecuting Christians.
Adversary	Mozart (God)	Christof (God)	Christians (God)
Flaw	Vainglory. He bargains with God on his own terms.	Innocence—he trusts people too easily. Also, fear of water.	Self-righteousness
Apparent Defeat	Salieri reads Mozart's music written on first pass and realizes that he does not have greatness in himself.	The big storm at sea, which is the final and most difficult barrier for Truman to face.	The Christian church grew faster than Paul could persecute them.
Final Confrontation	Salieri tries to "write" Mozart to death.	Truman debates with Christof, who is in the sky.	Damascus road experience—God wins.
Self-Revelation	He cannot win against God.	His life has been controlled by another. He must give up his security if he is to have freedom from another's control.	Paul realized that he was actually fighting against the very God he claimed to serve. His self-righteousness blinded him.
Resolution	Salieri refuses to submit and goes insane.	Truman walks out of his TV world through the stairway into freedom and uncertainty.	Paul ends up on trial for convincing people of the very thing he was trying to stop. But he is free from slavery to sin.

Figure 2. Elements of three stories

Another popular form of redemption is called "existentialism." This is the view that humanity exists in an ultimately irrational universe without meaning that leads to despair (angst). The way of redemption is through the acceptance of responsibility for creating ourselves through personal choice or commitment. *Forrest Gump* (1994) is the popular form of this redemption. Other existentialist movies include *Zelig* (1983), *Crimes and Misdemeanors* (1989), *City Slickers* (1991), *Groundhog Day* (1993), *Legends of the Fall* (1994), *Babe* (1995) and others. This existential redemption will be explored in more detail in chapter three.

Another increasingly popular redemption in film is Eastern mysticism. Mysticism takes many forms, of which the two strongest are monism and dualism.

Dualism is the *Star Wars* variety of redemption—the dark and light sides of the Force. *Ghost* (1990) offers a dualism in which the bad people get sucked into spiritual punishment and the good people, who embrace their light side by letting go of their control over others, enter Nirvana. This kind of dualism is salvation by good works.

Phenomenon (1996) and *Powder* (1995) are strong examples of the monistic view of redemption, the belief that enlightenment comes through experiencing a oneness with all things. This monist enlightenment will be discussed in detail in chapter five.

Another kind of redemption is the Christian notion of substitutionary sacrifice, faith, repentance and forgiveness. This one is extremely rare in movies—no surprise there, given the animosity many in Hollywood feel toward this dominant influence on Western civilization. Every once in a while movies like *Chariots of Fire* (1981), *Tender Mercies* (1983), *The Mission* (1986), *Shadowlands* (1993), *The Addiction* (1995) or *Les Misérables* (1998) come along and portray Christian redemption in their characters. Some of these will be discussed in chapter six, but suffice it to say that they all illustrate Christian redemption through motifs that encompass facing one's own moral guilt, the need for repentance, the cleansing power of forgiveness, the undeserved nature of grace, the substitutionary nature of atonement and freedom through dying to self. And there are many other elements of the Christian worldview, including loving one's neighbor, truth, justice, mercy and so on, all of which point toward or illustrate our inner need for redemption.

As a further qualification, not all stories of redemption are complete and deeply woven philosophies. Often they point to simple values like self-worth based on self-acceptance and not peer approval *(Toy Story,* 1995), coming-of-age being based on awareness of mortality and not sexuality *(My Dog Skip,* 2000; *Hearts in Atlantis,* 2001) or the dangers of trusting technology *(Terminator 2,* 1991; *Jurassic Park,* 1993). But even these values are ultimately about how we ought or ought not to live in this life, that is, redemption.

Join the Revolution

And so the story goes. Movies are finally, centrally, crucially, primarily, *only* about story. And those stories are finally, centrally, crucially, primarily, *mostly* about redemption. With the proper tools in hand, one can accurately and objectively discern the messages, worldviews and philosophies of life promoted in the movies. The enjoyment of entertainment need not result in thoughtless abdication of one's critical faculties to the manipulation of emotion. When asked what you think about a movie, you can now avoid the generic responses "I liked it" and "I didn't like it" and offer a more informed response that articulates the redemption portrayed in the story. Movies are, after all, not *only* movies.

Watch and Learn

1. Write out the nine basic elements of story structure from this chapter on a pad of paper. Then watch three films: a romantic comedy, a serious drama and an action movie. Afterward, fill in what you think fulfills each element for each movie.

2. Based on the character growth of the hero, write out the theme of each movie in the form of a moral and consider how the movie makes its argument to prove that moral. In what way do you agree or disagree with that theme? How might you have done it differently?

Part ②

Worldviews
in the Movies

③ Existentialism

Many people consider philosophy to be irrelevant to our everyday lives. It is something practiced by academic eggheads in remote ivory towers, but it is certainly not something that results in practical living or "real life."

Contrary to this negative perception, the late Francis Schaeffer often pointed out that philosophy, though considered irrelevant by many people, was often a pertinent driving force of culture. The ideas generated by academic thinkers filter down through the high arts into the popular arts and are thus consumed by the masses, often without self-conscious recognition of their philosophical nature.[1]

People may not call their philosophical beliefs by their academic names of metaphysics (reality), epistemology (knowledge) and ethics

---

[1]Francis Schaeffer, *The God Who Is There* (Downers Grove, Ill.: Intervarsity Press, 1968), pp. 13-48.

(morality), but they operate upon them nevertheless. When a person says that someone ought not butt in line at a movie theater (ethics) because everyone knows (epistemology) that "first come, first served" is the way the world works and that "what goes around, comes around" (metaphysics), then knowingly or unknowingly she is expressing a philosophy. When a kid watches the animated movie *Shrek,* he probably doesn't know about Carl Jung's theories of psychological types and the collective unconscious, but he is ingesting them nonetheless through those characters and that story adapted after the Jungian model.[2]

Everybody operates upon a philosophy in life, a worldview that defines for them the way the world works and how they know things and how they ought to behave. So philosophy is ultimately a practical reality for all of us. In this sense, everyone is a philosopher; some are just more aware of it than others.

Director's Cut

Visit ‹www.godawa.com› for further reading on the basics of worldview thinking.

One of the dominant influences on movies today is the philosophy of existentialism. In order to understand this influence, it is helpful to see the philosophy in its historical origins and context. In *Postmodern Times: A Christian Guide to Contemporary Thought and Culture,* Gene Edward Veith Jr. gives a brief outline to historical stages of thought in our Western civilization in order to show us how we got where we are now. He explains that the "premodern" phase, which included the Greek, Roman and early Christian empires, was marked by a recognition that reality was created and sustained by a supernatural realm beyond the senses. People believed in the supernatural and considered themselves subservient to it.[3]

By the 1700s, with the rise of the Renaissance culminating in the

---

[2]The screenwriters admit *Shrek*'s Jungian ideas: "The book is very clever, because it knowingly used Jungian symbolism to tell the story," said Ted Elliott. "That was the most important thing that we wanted to take from the book—that *subversiveness"* ("Movie News—June 1, 2001," Videomoviehouse.com <www.videomoviehouse.com/June-01-2001.php>, emphasis mine).

[3]Gene Edward Veith Jr., *Postmodern Times: A Christian Guide to Contemporary Thought and Culture* (Wheaton, Ill.: Crossway, 1994), pp. 27-32.

Enlightenment, society became "modern." That is, it began to see religion as ignorant, magical interpretations of a universe that is actually generated and sustained by naturalistic, machinelike laws, understood without any relation to deity. *Enlightenment* was the self-designation by this generation of humanists, who perceived the previous medieval era to be the "Dark Ages" precisely because religion was the dominant worldview, the "queen of the sciences." So their prejudicial language conferred the oppressive term "Dark Ages" in order to demonize their enemies. The so-called "Age of Reason" was marked by naturalistic science and autonomous reason as absolute tools for truth. Man was the measure of all things, and reason was his god.[4]

Voices of dissent against the juggernaut of Enlightenment tradition were raised in the Romanticism of the early nineteenth century. And Romantic ideas became the seeds of our current postmodern condition. As Veith explains,

> Whereas the Enlightenment assumed that reason is the most important human faculty, romanticism assumed that emotion is at the essence of our humanness. The romantics exalted the individual over the impersonal, abstract systems. Self-fulfillment, not practicality was the basis for morality. . . . Romantics criticized "civilization" as reflecting the artificial abstractions of the human intellect. Children are born free, innocent, and one with nature. "Society" then corrupts them with the bonds of civilization. . . . Romanticism cultivated subjectivity, personal experience, irrationalism, and intense emotion. . . . The romantics drew on Kant, who argued that the external world owes its very shape and structure to the organizing power of the human mind, which imposes order on the chaotic data of the senses. Some romantics took this to imply that the self, in effect, is the creator of the universe.[5]

Within this romantic milieu, existentialism was born.

---

[4]Man as the measure of all things was a concept originated by the ancient Greek philosopher Protagoras. In some ways, the Enlightenment was similar to the Renaissance, which heralded a return to the classical Greek forms and principles of thought.

[5]Veith, *Postmodern Times,* pp. 35-36.

A Necessarily Oversimplified Brief Introduction to Existentialism

Existentialism is a worldview that has many heads. So many varieties exist that it would take a book to define them all. There are even religious forms of existentialism to which some Christians lay claim. Famous translator and historian of existentialist philosophy Walter Kaufmann sums it up:

> Existentialism is not a school of thought nor reducible to any set of tenets.
> . . . The refusal to belong to any school of thought, the repudiation of the adequacy of any body of beliefs whatever, and especially of systems, and a marked dissatisfaction with traditional philosophy as superficial, academic, and remote from life—that is the heart of existentialism.[6]

Though some of the best-known modern thinkers who have espoused existentialism are Jean-Paul Sartre (1905-1980), Albert Camus (1913-1960) and Karl Jaspers (1883-1969),[7] its roots can largely be traced back to two men: Søren Kierkegaard (1813-1855), a Christian, and Friedrich Nietzsche (1844-1900), an atheist. We will address some of the specific beliefs of these men later in relation to particular films. For now I would like to focus on three emphases of the existential worldview in films today: (1) chance over destiny, (2) freedom over rules and (3) experience over reason.

Director's Cut

**Visit ‹www.godawa.com›
for further reading on
existentialism.**

Chance over Destiny

Existentialism accepts the Enlightenment notion of an eternally existing materialistic universe with no underlying meaning or purpose. While it does not deny the laws of nature, it sees these laws as order without purpose or meaning. This is what "the death of God" concept means—God

---

[6]Walter Kaufmann, *Existentialism from Dostoevsky to Sartre* (1956; reprint, Cleveland: World, 1970), back cover.

[7]In his *Existentialism,* Kaufmann adds to this list Dostoevsky, Rilke, Kafka and Heidegger.

does not "die" in the traditional sense, rather he ceases to be relevant because, without meaning behind the universe, the concept of God is unnecessary.

The universe may be uniform, but its uniformity appears to our human perspective as a product of chance. And chance ultimately defies any notion of destiny or a fixed purpose toward which things are headed. Within our human perspective, *anything,* in this sense, is ultimately possible.

With the advent of quantum physics, the notion of chance as the underlying reality of our mechanistic universe has become even more fashionable. Natural uniformity then becomes something that the mind imposes on a chaotic universe. Since this universe has no inherent meaning, we lead ourselves to despair if we try to find any meaning within it. The mechanical cause-and-effect universe does not fit our human desires and thus appears to us as absurd.

Forrest Gump (1994) and its predecessor *Being There* (1979) are both popular movies that communicate the idea of a chance world in which events occur without purpose. The use of mentally challenged men in both films is a metaphor for chance itself. They have no "intelligent design" to their lives and yet both of them become important figures in history without even realizing it.

In *Being There* Chance the gardener (a name chosen without coincidence) influences the president of the United States because Chance's simple-minded regurgitations of television platitudes are misinterpreted by accident as profound mysteries of genius. *Forrest Gump* has basically the same effect, with a simple-minded Forrest changing American history without even knowing it in a virtual exploration of the dual opposites of chance and destiny.

 **Director's Cut**

Take a deeper look at existentialism by reading my "Forrest Gump: Existentialism for the Common Man" at ‹www.godawa.com›.

The title for the movie *Being There* is an English translation of the German word *dasein,* used by German existentialist Martin Heidegger

(1889-1976) to define a human being as a field of probability, as opposed to the rationalist view of us as clear and distinct entities. At the last shot of *Being There,* just when we think there is some rational explanation for why this simple man has attained such status and impact on the world, he walks away from us on the surface of a lake—an allusion to the concept that mindless chance does in fact mysteriously guide the universe, like a god.

Grand Canyon (1991)—a drama from the pen of Lawrence Kasdan, who brought us the angst-ridden ensemble piece *The Big Chill* (1983)— is another strong picture of a chance-ruled universe. In the first half of the movie, its characters struggle with the randomness of good and evil in the world. Steve Martin plays a Hollywood director of mindless, violent action movies who gets randomly mugged and shot himself, then reconsiders making movies of substance and meaning because of his brush with death. In the very first scene he tells Kevin Kline's character, Mack, "Nothing can be controlled. We live in chaos, the central issue in everyone's life."

This sets the stage for the rest of the movie, which is filled with the random evils of life, from cut fingers and earthquakes to a neighbor's heart attack and drive-by shootings. And police search helicopters and siren-screaming ambulances (symbols of the chaos) are ubiquitously in the background.

Danny Glover's character, Simon, explains to Mack that people live by habit; we don't change. Hoping that our actions have meaning beyond us is hopeless. The conclusion of the film is found in Simon's personal vision of standing on the edge of the Grand Canyon, where "we realize what a big joke we all are, our big heads thinking what we do is going to matter all that much." His conclusion is that we are all like gnats that land on the rump of a cow chewing its cud next to a road you ride by at seventy miles an hour. A pretty concise summary of the existential dilemma of meaninglessness (absurdity).

As in Heidegger's "being unto death," Sartre's "nausea" and Kierkegaard's "crisis of dread," these characters, through their near-death experiences, face the anxiety of their meaningless existence. And this is what the existentialist term "dread" (angst) means. It is not merely fear itself or a specific fear, even of death, but rather the general, overwhelming revelation of the meaninglessness of our existence. A specific encounter with death merely triggers this self-revelation.[8]

The characters at moments wonder if all the chance happenings are miracles or messages from somewhere, maybe even sent by angels. But no answer is forthcoming from the supernatural. God is silent, because he is dead. They struggle with trying to make sense out of the pain and suffering in their lives but can ultimately find no rational answer. Fate and luck are ultimately what they believe in, condemning them to freedom in a random universe. Only by making individual choices to love other human beings do the characters connect with any personal redemption in the midst of chaos.

Two other films that attempt to show the absurdity of a determined universe without humanity's autonomous freedom are *Rosencrantz and Guildenstern Are Dead* (1990) and *The Music of Chance* (1993). They both have characters that are controlled by outside forces, making their lives meaningless labor leading to an equally meaningless death. Life becomes "sound and fury, signifying nothing."

The existentialist writer Albert Camus wrote of the Greek myth of Sisyphus, condemned to endlessly rolling a stone up a hill, only to have it roll back down again. He says of this symbol for our quest that "his passion for life won him that unspeakable penalty in which the whole being is exerted in accomplishing nothing."[9]

To be fair, there is some measure of truth to the claim that we cannot control the world around us and that we all need to see that our own self-inflated sense of significance and power is a delusion. The search for meaning behind the pain and suffering in the world is a noble pursuit.

---

[8]Alasdair MacIntyre, "Kierkegaard, Søren Aabye," in *The Encyclopedia of Philosophy,* ed. Paul Edwards (New York: Macmillan, 1972), p. 338.
[9]Albert Camus, *The Myth of Sisyphus and Other Essays* (New York: Random House, 1955), p. 89.

The seemingly random nature of evil is an honest problem for the human mind that merits the kind of consideration these films give it. But the ironic thing about such films expressing the notion of a chance universe is that they are written by writers who follow specific, predetermined rules of structure for storytelling.

Structure within a story means that everything that occurs within the story follows a preexisting plan, that is, an order with a purpose. One of the rules in effective filmmaking is that everything that happens in a movie has to have a purpose. From what a person eats to what is going on in the background are all precisely ordained by writer and director to communicate character, plot and theme. There can be no arbitrary events. Anything that does not advance the story must be thrown out.

In this way, the act of storytelling itself denies the notion of a chance universe without purpose. In order to communicate an idea about mindless indeterminacy, a writer would have to intelligently determine all the instances of "chance" occurrence in his story. He would be assuming as true what he is trying to prove false. So a determined universe is inescapable in the art of story. Yet a determined universe makes freedom, history and change philosophically impossible. Proposing that both chance and destiny are ultimately true is contradictory and self-refuting. So where's the balance? What kind of determination is true? The answer is in the storytelling.

The biblical view of determination is that a personal God (as opposed to impersonal fate) created the universe, and sovereignly controls and providentially destines all things that come to pass without forcing human beings against our wills or negating our responsibility (Romans 9). Storytelling reflects the Christian God and his providential determination of the free acts of human beings. A screenwriter providentially creates characters based on the kind of story he or she desires to tell. Authors determine every single word, every single act, good and evil, of all their characters, down to the jot and tittle, sometimes working for hours on just the right turn of a phrase or subtle plot twist. Even events that seem like chance occurrences in a movie, like a freak car accident or the lucky throw of dice, are deliberately written in by authors to direct the story exactly where they want it to go. Yet when an audience watches the movie, we see characters freely acting and morally accountable for their actions in a world where some things appear to happen by chance. Our knowing that the characters and their stories are predestined by an author does not make them any less valuable or their stories any less meaningful.

But this apparent free will and chance are shown by the end of the story to be parts of the ultimate self-revelation of the main characters and others—and that revelation was what the storyteller "predestined" in his orchestration of all the events. There is a plan to it all, even if the characters don't know it at the time. Thus storytelling reflects the ultimate storyteller of all history, God himself. In this way art becomes an apologetic.

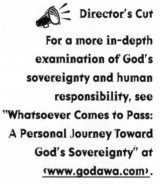

Director's Cut

For a more in-depth examination of God's sovereignty and human responsibility, see "Whatsoever Comes to Pass: A Personal Journey Toward God's Sovereignty" at ‹www.godawa.com›.

Magnolia

One film that addresses the freedom-determination debate in a decidedly biblical manner is *Magnolia* (1999), the Paul Thomas Anderson magnum opus, starring Tom Cruise, Julianne Moore and Jason Robards among others. It's the story of twelve-plus people whose lives intersect on one fateful evening during a storm of raining frogs. Each of them is embroiled in his or her own dysfunctional attempts to make sense of life and find some solace, as they are haunted by past pain and sins. The theme is revealed through a repeated phrase in the film: "We may be through with the past, but the past is not through with us." The power of the story lies in the reference to the underlying providence that drives them through apparent coincidences and into their respective redemptions.

The movie begins with a dramatization of several bizarre coincidences of history (which allegedly happened in real life). One is the story of how a scuba diver ended up on the top of a tree in a forest fire. Said scuba diver had just gone diving in a lake miles away from a forest fire. When a fire-fighting plane scooped up water from the lake to throw on the fire, the pilots were unaware that they had inadvertently scooped up the diver and so proceeded to dump him on burning trees.

Another is the fantastic tale of how a young man attempted suicide by jumping off a building, only to be accidentally shot on the way down by his mother, who was inside the building angrily pointing a rifle at his father. The rifle had "accidentally" gone off at the exact moment when the kid was flying by the window, hitting him and killing him. Irony of ironies, the kid would have survived the fall if he hadn't been shot, because he did not see the net that had been placed at the bottom of the building. And irony on top of irony on top of irony, he himself had loaded the usually unloaded rifle the night before! The narrator then explains in voice-over how he doesn't think these quirks of life are coincidences at all.

A common way of dealing with this kind of meaningful coincidence is to chalk it up to fate, an impersonal force that benevolently acts on our behalf *(Serendipity,* 2001; *Cast Away).* Fate here becomes a God-substitute. But *Magnolia* does not take this path of least resistance. Anderson goes out of his way to express *biblical* providence.

References to Bible verses occur throughout the movie. They are planted on billboards, whispered randomly by characters and even plastered on signs in a TV show audience. One is Exodus 34:7, which states, "[The LORD God] keeps lovingkindness for thousands, . . . forgives iniquity, transgression and sin; yet He will by no means leave the guilty unpunished, visiting the iniquity of fathers on the children and on the grandchildren to the third and fourth generations." The other is Exodus 8:2 which states, "If you refuse to let them go, behold, I will smite your whole territory with frogs." The entire film is about characters suffering under the negative effects of the sins of their fathers, which directly affect their own lives: overachievement, unfair expectations, abandonment, even incest. One of the two pure-hearted souls in this story loaded with foul-mouthed reprobates is a bumbling yet ultimately pure-hearted Christian cop (the other one being a compassionate nurse). But most of the other characters avoid facing their own culpability in the process. That is, until a freak rainstorm of frogs occurs that operates as a divine intervention in all their lives with intersecting velocity.

Ironically, when one considers Anderson's own explanation of why he chose the biblical imagery of frogs as well as the Bible verses to support it, one can only conclude that the making of this movie is an example of human freedom and divine determination. As Anderson explains:

> There's certainly a biblical reference there, but I'd be a liar if I said to you it was written initially as a biblical reference. I truthfully didn't even know it was in the Bible when I first wrote the sequence . . . but maybe there are certain moments in your life when things are so . . . confused that someone can say to you, "It's raining frogs," and that makes sense. That somehow makes sense as a warning; that somehow makes sense as a sign. I started to understand why people turn to religion in times of trouble, and maybe my form of finding religion was reading about rains of frogs and realizing that makes sense to me somehow. And then of course to discover it in the Bible and the reference that it makes there just sort of verifies it, like, "Hey, I guess I'm on the right track."[10]

Anderson's rejection of chance and his use of biblical providence is more arbitrary cultural imagery than true Christian devotion. But be that as it may, *Magnolia* is a film that illustrates that life is not a random sequence of unfortunate events but rather a providentially directed, divinely redeeming story. So it appears that Anderson is as much a subject of God's providence as are the characters in his own movie. *Magnolia* is a strong example of art imitating life.

Freedom over Rules

The existentialist's negation of systems and schools of thought is closely tied to the doctrine of the individual's personal freedom as opposed to external rules. If there is an underlying order to the universe, then we

---

[10]From an interview with Paul Thomas Anderson for *Creative Screenwriting Magazine,* posted on P. T. Anderson's website <www.ptanderson.com/articlesandinterviews/creative2000.htm>.

would all, by virtue of being part of that order or design, be automatons of fate. Law, be it nature or logic, is universal and unchanging. So true freedom necessitates that humans be unfettered by any external or internal laws or rules. This is what Sartre meant when he coined the phrase "Existence precedes essence"—we exist without any prior essence or fixed meaning.[11] Therefore, we human beings ought to create our own essence or meaning within that void by our free choices.

Sartre said we are "condemned to be free" because we want to have rules or order to give our lives meaning, yet there are none, and this is unsettling to the core of our being. Thus we are solely responsible for whatever happens in our lives. With absolute freedom comes absolute responsibility. Because we create our own lives by our own choices, we cannot blame what happens to us on anyone or anything else but ourselves. Responsibility for our actions is not the same idea for an existentialist as it is for a classical or Christian thinker.

In this view, since the universe is absurd, we cannot comfort ourselves by conformity to some external order like religion or philosophy. We must create our own meaning, create ourselves, create our own essence. Another way of saying this is that individual choice is our "self-creation." All external absolutes, all systems of order—be they moral, political or religious—are simply systems of slavery created by others, denying the individual's ultimate autonomous freedom in a chance universe.

If we vie for the safety of conformity to others' standards, we have exerted what Sartre called "bad faith";[12] or as scholar Walter Kaufmann translated it, "self-deception."[13] Since we are left to our own devices in order to define ourselves and create our essence, then we must look within ourselves to our personal intuition, our personal experience to make "good faith" choices.

Besides the "controlling" nature of morality and social norms, the ulti-

---

[11]Alasdair MacIntyre, "Essence and Existence," in *The Encyclopedia of Philosophy,* ed. Paul Edwards (New York: Macmillan, 1972), p. 60.

[12]Jean-Paul Sartre, *Essays in Existentialism* (New York: Citadel, 1993), pp. 147-86.

[13]Kaufmann, *Existentialism,* p. 222.

mate controller of all things is God. So it is no surprise that atheistic existentialism stresses "the death of God" and that religious existentialism stresses the "wholly otherness" of God. A "wholly other" God is a God who exists on a plane irrelevant to our rational scientific world, a God who can be encountered only by an irrational "leap of faith."

A good example of a film about freedom over rules is *Pleasantville* (1998), written and directed by Gary Ross. It's the story of two 1990s Gen-Xers (brother and sister) who find themselves magically transported into the world of an old black-and-white TV show called *Pleasantville*. The obvious intent of the filmmakers here is to attack traditional morality as embodied in the 1950s *Ozzie and Harriet* mentality, which is portrayed as oppressive to the individual's freedom. "Black-and-white people" discover joy and turn into color when they make personal choices against society's norms. Most of these choices wind up being for premarital and adulterous sex, an expression of freedom through immorality.

In one scene a girl plucks a "colored" apple off a tree to eat—a symbolic pointer to the Fall in Eden as a positive growth for humanity. By choosing to eat the fruit, Adam and Eve were actually taking an enlightened step of maturity, making their own moral choices rather than following the rigid "traditional morality" imposed by God.

Pleasantville does not merely attack morals but also offers the proposition that *all* external norms are oppressive and that redemption is found in people making their own internal, individual choices. The promiscuous sister finds her redemption, after turning half the schoolgirls into happy whores, by choosing to hunker down and bury her head in the books to secure a real education. The key to her redemption lies not in making a moral decision but in making her own decision apart from any external rules.[14]

---

[14]This same absoluteness of "personal choice" is broached as a theme in the film *Citizen Ruth* (1996), written by Alexander Payne and Jim Taylor. Laura Dern is Ruth, a pregnant, drug-addicted, unwed mother who is fought over by both pro-life people and pro-choice people. The conclusion of the story is that she walks away from both camps because each violates her freedom to direct her own life. All external value systems err in imposing obligations to any code of behavior, liberal *or* conservative.

A good example of a movie that counters the exaltation of autonomous freedom and rejection of traditional family values is *Blast from the Past* (1999), written by Bill Kelly and Hugh Wilson. This fish-out-of-water fairy tale of a 1960s family who mistakenly live in a bomb shelter for thirty-five years is an upside-down version of *Pleasantville*. A young man who has grown up in the shelter finally comes out one day into the 1990s and meets and falls in love with a young girl. The *Ozzie and Harriet* family values of chivalry and virtue that are ridiculed by modern society are all this boy knows. And it is precisely those values that make him the individual with the most quality and character in the angst-ridden, cynical, lawless world around him. Innocence and purity are elevated as virtue rather than embarrassment.

Woody Allen: Auteur of Nihilism

Nihilism is a particular vein of existentialist antiphilosophy that has its origins in Friedrich Nietzsche's writings. It is noted for its emphasis on the meaninglessness of existence because of the inability to rationally justify moral standards external to humanity.[15] Although despair is a common disposition of nihilists, Nietzsche used it as his steppingstone to propose that individuals should optimistically create their own morality in the vacuum that is left. As Kaufmann notes, the genetic influence of Nietzsche's thought on existentialism is profound,[16] and so is his influence on Woody Allen. Let's look at the themes that dominate this Nietzschean evangelist of nihilism.

Many of Allen's films, like *Annie Hall* (1977), *Manhattan* (1979), *Stardust Memories* (1980), *Hannah and Her Sisters* (1986), *Bullets over Broadway* (1994) and *Deconstructing Harry* (1997) are chock full of angst-filled searches for significance and "final experiences" resolved in characters accepting their insignificant place in the universe or self-destructing.

---

[15]Robert G. Olson, "Nihilism," *Encyclopedia of Philosophy*, p. 517.
[16]Kaufmann, *Existentialism*, p. 100.

Zelig (1983) is a comedy about a little guy with a bizarre psychological dysfunction who takes on the physical traits of those he is around. He ends up meeting historical figures like Stalin, Hitler, Churchill and others, and we see him looking like each one of them. This is a fable about a guy who has to realize that he has a problem with being "others-directed" and that he can only find redemption when he becomes "inner-directed" or "self-directed"—another Nietzschean theme. Allen Bloom, the distinguished political philosopher, notes:

> Woody Allen's comedy is nothing but a set of variations on the theme of the man who does not have a real "self" or "identity," and feels superior to the inauthentically self-satisfied people because he is conscious of his situation and at the same time inferior to them because they are "adjusted." This borrowed psychology turns into a textbook in *Zelig,* which is the story of an "other-directed" man, as opposed to an "inner-directed" man, terms popularized in the 1950s by David Riesman's *The Lonely Crowd,* borrowed by him from his analyst, Erich Fromm, who himself absorbed them (for example, *innige Mensch*) from a really serious thinker, Nietzsche's heir, Martin Heidegger.[17]

Bloom concludes with astonishment at how doctrinaire Woody Allen's "Americanized nihilism"—a nihilism based on a profound German philosophy—has become in the American entertainment market.

Crimes and Misdemeanors (1989) marks the high point of Allen's crusade of nihilism. Martin Landau plays an upstanding doctor who struggles with guilt over his adultery and consequent hired murder of his mistress. His rabbi, who counsels him in spiritual matters, is going blind, symbolizing the blind faith and inadequacy of religion.

Allen himself plays a filmmaker doing a documentary on a Jewish existentialist theologian wrestling with the evil in the world. Landau remembers his dinner-table family discussions as a child in which his

---

[17]Allan Bloom, *The Closing of the American Mind: How Higher Education Has Failed Democracy and Impoverished the Souls of Today's Students* (New York: Simon & Schuster, 1987), p. 144.

religious and atheist relatives argued over the Holocaust. The conclusion: there is no God; there is only the will to power. The reason why Hitler lost was not because he was wrong but because the Allies were stronger. Might makes right, the ghost of Nietzsche forever haunting celluloid.

At the end of the film Landau relieves his conscience by recognizing

Director's Cut

Visit ‹www.godawa.com› for further reading on Friedrich Nietzsche.

that "in the absence of a god, man assumes responsibility for his own actions." By freeing himself from the external oppression of religious guilt, in a "tragic" freedom he carves his own future and so the past guilt fades away. Condemned to be free, because all guilt is, after all, the product of an artificial pressure by an external code of conduct that violates our ultimate autonomy, the character gets away with murder and purges his conscience in the process.

In true existential expression of the ultimate control over the self, the Jewish theologian commits suicide. To conclude the film Allen gives a final statement about life fitting of Nietzsche himself:

We are all faced throughout our lives with agonizing decisions—moral choices. Some are on a grand scale. Most of these choices are on lesser points. But we define ourselves by the choices we make. We are the sum total of our choices. Events unfold so unpredictably, so unfairly. Human happiness does not seem to be included in the design of creation. It is only we with our capacity to love that give meaning to the indifferent universe. Most human beings seem to have the ability to keep trying, and even to find joy from simple things, like their family, their work, and from the hope that future generations might understand more.

In other words, morality and conscience are not objective reflections of the underlying moral order created by God, but rather are a function of the human being who creates meaning in a meaningless, amoral universe. This struggle with the origin of conscience as rooted in society and the desire to rid oneself of guilt from immoral behavior is a common theme in Allen's movies, and not surprisingly, in his personal life as well. After all, ideas do have consequences.

Seven

And speaking of consequences, a disturbingly profound movie that addresses the negative results of existential relativity is the thriller *Seven* (1995), written by Andrew Kevin Walker and starring Brad Pitt and Morgan Freeman. Many consider this film to be too gruesome to watch, though in fact almost nothing is shown of the actual violence. Like a good novel (and the Bible) most of the evil acts are left up to the imagination.

In *Seven*, the killer, after being caught for his murders based on the seven deadly sins from Dante's *Inferno*, explains to the two detectives that by ignoring moral absolutes, society has actually bred the worst of evils. A world that no longer believes in sin no longer has authority to distinguish moral differences or condemn the worst of villainy. This movie, in which the killer is actually philosophically correct, makes us look at ourselves to see the monsters we have become.[18] In the nineteenth century we witnessed the "death of God"; in the twentieth century we witnessed its consequence—the death of humanity.[19]

Many people avoid these kinds of gritty serial-killer thrillers because of their darkness. And in fact, many of them *are* exploitative. But if done properly, movies in this genre can offer some of the most ringing indict-

---

[18]The writer of *Seven*, Andrew Walker, did not necessarily intend a Christian worldview in his script. In fact, he may have been attacking Christianity in his portrayal of the means "religious" people will use to "cleanse" society of perceived evils. Some of Walker's other movies, among them *Sleepy Hollow* and *8MM*, support an anti-Christian prejudice. Even so, *Seven* serves as an example of an argument that unwittingly illuminates the superiority of the counterargument. People who say morality is relative or socially constructed have no right to complain when someone acts as though morality is relative or socially constructed. Ideas have consequences.

[19]An older movie with this same sort of scathing indictment of existential morality is *Rope* (1948) by Alfred Hitchcock. Jimmy Stewart plays a professor of Nietzschean philosophy who has his own ideas turned against him when a couple of students use those ideas to justify murdering another student. Stewart comes to terms with the fact that his ideas have consequences and that morality is true and necessary.

ments of the falsity of belief in the goodness of human nature. Because serial killers are often intelligent and well educated, they shatter the Enlightenment belief that the smarter we become, the more virtuous we are. But it also casts doubt on contemporary psychological theories of criminal insanity. True insanity could not possibly be so utterly rational, which means such behavior is deliberate evil.

Experience over Reason

Existentialism repudiates the abstract reasoning of traditional philosophy as superficial, preferring instead the concrete realm of experience. To the existentialist, reason, as the ultimate ordering system in a godless universe, is the most overused, overvalued tool. The modernists thought that through science, logic and careful rational reflection we would discover the underlying order to all things. But we cannot find such order or meaning in a chance universe. Reasoning only leads to despair (angst). We cannot find meaning through reason; we must *create* meaning through our own choices and experience.

This rejection of reason as a means of discovering truth in favor of "experience" results in an inward-looking heart-over-head outlook. Intuition (feelings) takes precedence over logic. And this is what Kierkegaard meant when he said that truth is subjectivity.[20] Truth is not something outside of us that we discover through cold, impersonal propositions, but rather it is something we experience subjectively, inwardly, in a personal way. This inwardness is also referred to as "encountering" or "appropriating" a personal relationship with truth, as opposed to mere mental assent, and it is marked by the raw commitment of the will.[21]

---

[20]Søren Kierkegaard, *Concluding Unscientific Postscript,* trans. David F. Swenson and Walter Lowrie (Princeton, N.J.: Princeton University Press, 1941), p. 116.

[21]The existential emphasis on volitional choice as what defines us is the belief that we are what we do. We are not so much "beings" as we are "becomings." Our acts, not our thoughts, doctrines or ideas, define us. We are the sum total of our choices and experiences. This is more than a philosophical translation of the common proverb "Actions speak louder than words"; it is an outright rejection of humanity's identity as having any essence outside of our choices or commitments. Because existence precedes essence, we create meaning for our lives (essence) through our individual choices and experiences.

The idea of following your heart, instead of following your head or doing your duty, is the driving force of many a movie character's self-revelations.[22] It is a common and explicitly stated theme in such movies as *A Time to Kill* (1996), *Jefferson in Paris* (1997), *Meet Joe Black* (1998), *The Mask of Zorro* (1998), *Mulan* (1998), *Star Wars: The Phantom Menace* (1999), *Crazy in Alabama* (1999), *Bicentennial Man* (1999) and *Hercules* (1999).

The worldwide megablockbuster to end all blockbusters, *Titanic,* is a gigantic expression of this rejection of social norms in favor of personal intuition, or the heart-over-head approach. James Cameron uses the post-Victorian setting of the early twentieth century, with all its traditional propriety and alleged repression, to express a defiant existential romanticism.

The heroine, Rose, is oppressed by a controlling and violent fiancé, Cal, the epitome of the worst of a patriarchal aristocratic society. To the modern mindset, male headship leads *only* to oppression and violence, and so Cal is a male oppressor. Rose's redemption is found in rejecting her obligations to these social norms and choosing her own future by following her heart.

To be sure, the violent Cal is an undesirable mate for Rose. But love in this story is not the rational choice to submit oneself to another *trustworthy* person. Rather it is the irrational resignation to one's intuitive feelings. Jack has Rose stand at the front of the ship and then close her eyes and release her grip to "feel" the freedom of letting go. When they dance, he tells her, "Just move with me. Don't think." When Rose disagrees with Cal over a Picasso painting (a postmodern artist), she tells him, "There's truth without logic." And that truth is in the heart.

When Rose first talks with Jack about her dreams, she wishes she

---

[22]Michael Medved is the one to thank for this concept of "follow your heart over doing your duty" in the movies. I first heard him point this out on his radio talk show and took a shine to it because, of course, it's true. He expounded how movies of yesteryear tended to emphasize doing one's duty over following the heart. I have added the interpretation of this springing from our existentialism-infected culture.

could just "chuck it all and become an artist, poor but free," or maybe "a dancer like Isadora Duncan, a wild, pagan spirit." Here is a romantic, feminist longing. She envies "wandering Jack" because he lives the free-spirited life of an artiste—he is poor but having fun, living a moment-by-moment, experience-by-experience existence. Jack's buddies fret over his impossible desire for the aristocratic Rose. "He's not being logical," says one. "Amoré is'a not logical," replies the other. Indeed Jack is not logical, because he is a man who lives by his heart. This "king of the world" is the incarnation of the existential man. And when he is implicated in stealing Cal's huge diamond, Rose chooses to believe Jack against all evidence. *She listens to her heart.* At the end of the story, she says that Jack saved her "in every way that a person can be saved," because he not only saved her physically but also freed her from the oppression of her social norms.

To be fair, Jack did save Rose from an oppressive marriage and from the nightmare of living a false life determined by others. As the pictures on her bedside at the end illustrate, because of Jack she would go on to experience the things she longed for: horseback riding like a man (not side-saddle) at the Santa Monica pier, flying a plane like a man (traditionally, a male adventure) and even living a romantic life (as the glamour portrait indicates). And in the final shot we see Rose die and find her way to "heaven" in the arms of her ultimate savior and redeemer: Jack—as she remembered him. To find such love of another human is the highest aspiration in this film, the chief end of man.

The literary genius of *Titanic* lies in Cameron's ability not merely to tell an interesting love story but also to incarnate the change of an era into the characters and even the ship itself. The story is used as a metaphor for the death of traditional order (patriarchy) and the rise of egalitarianism, with a new existential ethos of personal autonomy. Cal and his stuffy, aristocratic, old-order bunch are controllers of women and proud of their intellectual power, which is dying under the weight of its own pride. It is not without irony that this existentialist tale of liberation should take place on the "unsinkable" Titanic, the highest achievement of humankind's "unsinkable" rationality and order, the fruit of the Enlightenment and resultant Industrial Revolution.

Following one's heart instead of one's head is a common idea in most romance movies. It often involves the pairing of a rigid, rules-oriented person with an unpredictable, free-spirited partner, thus making room for dramatic conflict and humor. Some examples of this freedom through defiance are *One Flew over the Cuckoo's Nest* (1975), *Romancing the Stone* (1984), *Ferris Bueller's Day Off* (1986), *What About Bob?* (1991), *Legends of the Fall* (1994), *Don Juan DeMarco* (1995), *Bridges of Madison County* (1995), *Tin Cup* (1996), *Box of Moonlight* (1996) and *Forces of Nature* (1999).

A Sensible Cure for Romanticism

A movie that presents a remedy to the Romantic obsession with the heart is *Sense and Sensibility* (1995), adapted by Emma Thompson from the Jane Austen novel. In the 1800s the word *sense* was a reference to the mannerly restraint of the mind, while *sensibility* referred to the passions. This dichotomy is played out in the two lead characters: Elinor (played by Emma Thompson) and Marianne (played by Kate Winslet).

Elinor, the mature, restrained one (representing sense), does not reveal her feelings readily. She is thoughtful and slow to speak but quick to listen. Her love for respectable young Edward is repressed because of his engagement to another woman and the potential for scandal. She refuses to let her passions interfere and break someone else's heart. So she patiently waits for another good man to come along.

Meanwhile, young and vivacious Marianne is a romantic (representing sensibility). She chides Elinor for her propriety: "Always prudence, honor, and duty. Elinor, where is your heart?" Marianne is in love with the idea of love, imbibing the passionate, romantic fury of young Willoughby, who is handsome, exciting, adventurous—and a fraud. Because of her slavery to her passions, Marianne fails to see this deception in Willoughby's treasure-seeking manipulation until it is too late and he dumps her, leaving her heartbroken and lost. She fails to see the steady and true love of the dedicated yet unflattering Colonel Brandon until she realizes that true love is commitment based on endurance and character, not feelings.

And Elinor receives her love in Edward after a long, painful loneliness when it turns out that Edward's engagement is broken. Their love for one another is finally expressed and Elinor breaks out into the most powerful display of weeping in the film. Hers is a heart properly held in check by the head.

In both cases, that of Elinor and of Marianne, the highest goal of true and abiding love is found in the restraint and subjugation of the emotions by the mind.

A Lesson from Grandfather

As mentioned earlier, one of the grandfathers of existentialism is Søren Kierkegaard. This melancholy nineteenth-century Danish philosopher is the famous source of the concept of the "leap of faith." The leap is necessary, according to Kierkegaard, because reason cannot be successful in finding the true meaning of life in the universe. Rationality goes only so far. You can't prove or disprove God and meaning in life, because such things are contradictory to the rational mind. They are beyond proof and can be understood only by an irrational commitment of faith *against* the evidence.

Kierkegaard believed that humanity has three stages of existence: the Aesthetic, the Ethical and the Religious.[23] The Aesthetic stage consists of a person in bondage to his passions. He is egocentric, living for the gratification of his pleasures. He seeks the fulfillment of his senses as a means of significance. But eventually he realizes that he can never get enough this way and is driven to despair (angst).

At this point, he takes a leap to the next phase, the Ethical. In the Ethical phase the person seeks discipline and order as a means of salvation. He commits to rules, obeying duty because he thinks that by order and

---

[23]These ideas are developed in his books *Either/Or* (1843) and *Fear and Trembling* (1843).

moral obligation he may attain the meaning he seeks. But the stress of this impossibility again leads to despair and to another leap into the final stage, the Religious.

When a person makes the final religious leap, he realizes full maturity and dependence upon his Creator through absolute devotion. This "purity of heart to will one thing," as Kierkegaard put it,[24] is marked by the suspension of the ethical by behavior that is normally condemned by society or even the conscience as immoral. But only by ignoring the mind can a person achieve the salvation he seeks. Kierkegaard used the example of God asking Abraham to kill his own son, Isaac, as the ultimate situation of the Religious Man, a person suspending his personal morals and understanding in order to find God.

Several movies of recent years are almost textbook examples of Kierkegaard. *Joe Versus the Volcano* (1990), *City Slickers* (1991), *Groundhog Day* (1993), *Unstrung Heros* (1995) and *Box of Moonlight* (1996) are just a few. In *City Slickers,* written by Lowell Ganz and Babaloo Mandell, three friends are trapped in the Aesthetic stage by their yearly pursuit of adrenaline highs at bull runs, scuba diving, baseball fantasy camp and target parachute jumping. Phil (Daniel Stern) engages in adultery because of his frigid, domineering wife. The youth- and sex-obsessed Ed (Bruno Kirby) is on a perpetual quest for younger women to bag. And Mitch (Billy Crystal) reaches a midlife crisis, wondering, "When is it ever going to be enough?" Phil and Ed are in the Aesthetic stage, while Mitch is an Ethical man, always doing the right thing, the moral thing (that is, not sleeping around), but still lacking meaning in life as death looms on his horizon.

Mitch decides to go on a cattle drive with the other two in order to "find his smile." When he does, he meets Curly (Jack Palance), a tough, mysterious cowboy possessing enigmatic wisdom. Mitch asks Curly what he thinks the secret to life is, and Curly raises his index finger and answers, "One thing." He says, "Stick to it, and the rest of life don't mean

---

[24]MacIntyre, *"Kierkegaard,"* p. 336.

a thing." When Mitch asks what the one thing is, Curly says, "That's what you've got to figure out."

After the long cattle drive, it finally hits Mitch that they were seeking the wrong thing all along. By trying to find out what the "one thing" is, they had missed the understanding that it isn't a specific one thing that they need; it's commitment to *any* one thing. It is single-minded devotion that satisfies the heart, not some external thing. This is Kierkegaardian commitment of the will—but without God.

In Danny Rubin's *Groundhog Day* (1993), Bill Murray plays a cynical weather reporter who gets stuck in living the same incredibly boring day over and over again (literally) in the worst hick town with the worst hick people he can imagine. As Sartre said, "Hell is other people."[25] This is an analogy for many who feel as if every day of their life is the same boring experience in which nothing really matters. Shades of Sisyphus. When he realizes this curse, he reacts by going through the three stages.

First, since the end of every day reverts to the day before, he decides to imbibe in selfish things, since he won't have to suffer consequences. He pigs out on unhealthy food, seduces as many women as he can, robs a Brinks car, same day after same day. This is the Aesthetic stage of complete abandonment to the flesh. The world becomes his playground. But this also becomes boring for him, and he is led to despair (angst) and starts killing himself in different ways, only to wake up alive again, as he was the day before.

Then he enters the Ethical stage by deciding to use his knowledge of events to do the moral thing, to help people. Every day he saves the same kid from falling out of a tree, the same man from choking on food in a restaurant. But this Messiah complex also leads to despair.

It is not until he decides to personally and selflessly love a woman (played by Andie McDowell) that he finds redemption. At first he uses his cumulative knowledge of her interests to woo her into bed, but then he realizes that his existence is not for himself but for selfless devotion to

---

[25]Jean-Paul Sartre, *No Exit and Three Other Plays* (New York: Alfred A. Knopf, 1955), p. 47.

another. Again, it's the Religious stage, including the same kind of commitment, but without God.

In John Patrick Shanley's *Joe Versus the Volcano* (1990), Joe (played by Tom Hanks), escapes his humdrum existence and certain death at an alienating, life-sucking job by going to a remote island and casting himself into a volcano. It's the story of a man who finds his identity by taking a "leap of faith." As his companion, Patricia (played by Meg Ryan), tells him, "We'll jump and we'll see what happens. That's life."

Qoheleth Speaks

Existentialism is the foundation of many modern movies. The reason it is so powerful an influence is precisely because it is partially true. It arrives at the inescapable conclusion of life's absurdity from the modern premise that there is no God and that we live in a chance universe. If there is no God, then there is no ultimate meaning to the universe. If there is no ultimate meaning, then we are truly alone, condemned to our freedom, forced to create our own meaning. God and all forms of external rules, like morality, are oppressive forms of control.

The book of Ecclesiastes addresses this condition of facing the angst of a world without meaning. The Preacher, Qoheleth, agrees with the existentialist, saying, "Behold, all is vanity and striving after wind" (Ecclesiastes 1:14). He tries to seek wisdom, but this leads to despair. "For there is no lasting remembrance of the wise man as with the fool, inasmuch as in the coming days all will be forgotten" (2:16). He experiments with the hedonistic pleasure-seeking of the Aesthetic but concludes again that "all was vanity and striving after wind and there was no profit under the sun" (2:11). He even embraces absurdity, madness and folly, but yet again a crisis encounter with death fills him with angst, for "the wise man's eyes are in his head, but the fool walks in darkness. And yet I know that one fate befalls them both" (2:14).

Yet the difference between the Preacher and the existentialist is the difference between redemption and resignation, heaven and hell. The existentialist concludes that in a godless universe all of our dreams and words are empty. Since there is no underlying meaning or creator, we create our own. The Preacher, on the contrary, concludes that we must return to the God we have ignored, for only then can the experience of life be made meaningful again. "For who can eat and who can have enjoyment without Him?" (2:25). "For in many dreams and in many words there is emptiness. Rather, fear God" (5:7). This is not a leap into the dark of an irrational void; it is a reasonable return to the God we knowingly rejected (Romans 1:18-23).

It is also instructive that this man of experience would conclude, after "all has been heard," that truly authentic existence is not found in freedom from rules but in following the warning to "fear God and keep His commandments, because this applies to every person. For God will bring every act to judgement, everything which is hidden, whether good or evil" (Ecclesiastes 12:13-14).

Watch and Learn

1. Have your small group read Ecclesiastes and then get together to watch *Groundhog Day*. What experiences do Bill Murray's character and the writer of Ecclesiastes share? In what ways does the movie differ in viewpoint from Ecclesiastes? Try to illustrate your answers with actual texts from Ecclesiastes. Discuss how Ecclesiastes balances the extremes of despair and hope.

2. Watch any one of the movies mentioned in this chapter and discuss how it deals with chance over destiny, freedom over rules and experience over reason. In what ways do you agree with the filmmakers, and in what ways do you disagree?

4 Postmodernism

Many cultural analysts point out that we are currently in a "post-modern" society.[1] This term indicates, among other things, a basic world-view that rejects absolutes—all absolutes, of any kind whatsoever. This is its simplest expression. In its more complex form it conjures up such complex technical terms as *deconstructionism, semiotics, metanarratives* and *totalizing discourses.* But ultimately it is the belief that there is no underlying objective reality or meaning to existence.[2]

As previously stated, the paradigm change in worldviews from the premodern to the modern was a transformation from a belief in reality

---

[1]Gene Edward Veith Jr. claims that the term *postmodern* was originally coined in the 1940s by famous historian Arnold Toynbee but that it became officially acknowledged by some in the early 1970s with the destruction of the Pruitt-Igoe housing development in St. Louis. See Gene Edward Veith Jr., *Postmodern Times: A Christian Guide to Contemporary Thought and Culture* (Wheaton, Ill.: Crossway, 1994), pp. 39, 44-45.

[2]Ibid., pp.15-18.

founded on the spiritual to a belief in reality founded on the rational. Even though these two stages of history could be considered hostile to one another, they still shared one commonality between them that is not shared with the postmodern paradigm of our current age: the belief in an objective reality. The premodern and the modern may have disagreed about the *nature* of reality, but at least they both believed that there *was* a reality and that it was incumbent upon people to discover that reality and align themselves with it. But with the coming of romanticism and existentialism came the lack of concern for any objective reality, replaced with a subjective interest in the human experience.

It is easy to see why the next step in philosophy would naturally be the denial of any objective reality whatsoever. The existential rejection of external rules became the will to power of the postmodern. The death of God became the death of reality itself. To be sure, there are significant differences between the two philosophies, such as the individualism of existentialism versus the collectivism of postmodernism, but as James W. Sire explains, "Existentialism is the philosophical basis for postmodernism."[3]

The two worldviews agree that since there is no underlying objective reality, then there is no absolute reference point to judge true and false, right and wrong, real and unreal. There is no ultimate order in the universe, no foundational reality. But whereas the existentialist idolized the individual as supreme, the postmodernist posits the loss of identity for the individual in favor of collective groups of people (cultures) constructing reality through their own interpretations and imposing them on others. And the way cultures do this is primarily through language.

Prison Houses of Language
Language can be a powerful tool to oppress people. One example is the use of euphemisms to justify evil deeds. A euphemism is an indirect word

---

[3]James W. Sire, *The Universe Next Door: A Basic Worldview Catalog* (Downers Grove, Ill.: InterVarsity Press, 1997), p. 38.

that is used in the place of a direct one in order to soften the impact and shape attitudes. In the antebellum South, for example, proslavery individuals described blacks as property in order to deny the humanity of those whom they were enslaving. In World War II the Nazis described their murdering of Jews as "the final solution" in order to deny the humanity of those whom they were murdering. Racists use derogatory animalistic words for their victims in order to deny the humanity of those whom they persecute. In a very real sense, the language of a culture shapes the thoughts and actions of that culture.

These cases illustrate the ways in which language can be a powerful tool for oppressing particular groups of people by reshaping the thoughts of a society and justifying evil deeds. The traditional understanding of language seeks to describe or refer to reality with a more accurate use of language. We correct bad language and beliefs with more objectively true language. So we call "the final solution" what it really is: a Holocaust of murder. And we call racism what it really is: damnable hatred. But the postmodern believes there is *no* objective reality, so any alteration of language is simply changing from one oppression to a different oppression. What we think is reality is actually a biased construct of our language. We "see" through the filter of our language. People are therefore trapped in "prison houses of language."[4]

Another commonality between the two philosophies of existentialism and postmodernism is the negation of reason as a means of discovering truth. But rather than merely rejecting the ability of reason to discover truth, as the existentialist did, the postmodern now rejects reason altogether as a "mask of power" that is used by one culture to enslave another. Reason becomes a means not of objective proof but of Western domination. The belief in objectivity actually objectifies people into tools for power. Binary thinking—right and wrong, true and false—is an exclusionary expression that must be overturned for a pluralistic decen-

---

[4]Of course, the negation of objective reality and referential language is itself an objective claim using referential language. For the proposition to be true, it would necessarily be false.

tralization of society into segments of constituent people groups.[5]

Postmodernists focus on deconstructing a belief into the various cultural prejudices that shaped it, rather than determining the verity of a truth claim. After all, if there is no truth or reality, then no belief or worldview *about* reality can be objectively true. Propositions about reality are reducible to personal agendas or biases. Postmoderns will even go so far as to say that personal identity is also an illusion, because we are constructed by our society. This is what is meant by the "death of the author." The individual identity of authors disappears when we uncover the social and cultural biases behind their viewpoints.

Director's Cut

For Christian analysis of postmodernism, see Gene Edward Veith Jr., *Postmodern Times: A Christian Guide to Contemporary Thought and Culture* (Wheaton, Ill.: Crossway, 1994); and Denis McCallum, ed., *The Death of Truth: What's Wrong with Multiculturalism, the Rejection of Reason and the New Postmodern Diversity* (Bloomington, Minn.: Bethany House, 1996). For further reading about postmodernism, visit ‹www.godawa.com›.

This "hermeneutics of suspicion" is pointed at what is called "metanarratives." Veith says, " 'Metanarratives' are stories about stories, 'large scale theoretical interpretations purportedly of universal application'; that is to say, *worldviews.* Postmodernism is a worldview that denies all worldviews."[6] In other words, worldviews, religions or even philosophies are simply extensive "stories" that we tell ourselves to create the world the way we want it to be.

And the postmodern emphasis is on story *as fiction.* Gone is the idea that any story is actually true. If there is no objective reality outside of ourselves, then all of our ideas of reality can only be fiction, rationalizations of our own prejudices. All stories are fiction, and most of them are pulp.

---

[5]This warring tribalism is why so much of postmodernism is "rage-oriented," because it is founded in the elevation of personal subjective emotions over objective rational truth. If there is no objective standard, then the one who speaks loudest wins.

[6]Veith, *Postmodern Times,* p. 49.

Pulp Fiction

Pulp Fiction (1994), Quentin Tarantino's pièce de résistance, marked the breaking and entering of postmodern filmmaking into the mainstream culture from its more independent, art-house and foreign film environment. It was the movie that started it all, and it did so with style.

Before *Pulp Fiction,* many movies have used the flashback as a technique to break up linear storytelling into a more interesting variety. But never had a mainstream film actually told a story mixed up out of sequence, showing the middle at the beginning, bouncing back and forth in time and even ending with a character's earlier life *after* showing his death. This negation of linear narrative created a whole new postmodern, nonlinear context for viewing story.

And the style of the film also embodies the eclecticism of postmodern fashion. In his book *Introducing Postmodernism,* author Richard Appignanesi points out the legacy of postmodern architecture on the broader art world as returning to ornament, "with references to the historic past and its symbolism, but in the ironic manner of parody, pastiche and quotation."[7] Postmodern art is an eclectic mix of styles, borrowing from all movements, all systems, maintaining no style of its own except for the hodgepodge of disparate elements amalgamated into a diverse whole.

There is no better description of *Pulp Fiction* than "pastiche." It revels in bad pop culture. The story takes place in an undisclosed time period that looks like the 1970s, with black Afros and long hair. The soundtrack is an eclectic mix of everything from Chuck Berry to the Tornados. We see *Clutch Cargo* cartoons (kitsch) and motorcycle exploitation films on the television, references to the Fonz from *Happy Days* and—the apex of it all—an entire sequence at a retro diner where waiters dress up like famous people in entertainment history, like Ed Sullivan and Marilyn Monroe.

Tarantino deliberately plays bad black-and-white city street rear pro-

---

[7]Richard Appignanesi, Ziauddin Sarder and Patrick Curry, *Introducing Postmodernism* (New York: Totem, 1998), p. 116.

jections behind his moving car scenes. He mocks the use of symbolic objects in movies by telling an outrageous story of a watch passed down as a family heirloom invested with deep sentiment because of all the trouble the father had protecting it to give to his son—he stuck it in his anus for five years in a POW camp during the war.

Tarantino gives a nod to multiculturalism by having at least three interracial romances among the main characters—an unusual occurrence in movies at the time. But also the lead hit man, Vincent (played by John Travolta), is always speaking of his three-year stay in Europe and how different European culture is from the American way of life. Tarantino, a self-confessed lover of pop culture, has even rereleased several of his favorite exploitation films of the seventies. Aware of it or not, he *is* a postmodern man.

And *Pulp Fiction* is a world without absolutes, without the finer distinction of good guys and bad guys. In fact, there really are no good guys at all. There are only differing levels of comparative badness. Butch, the two-timing, fight-fixing boxer, is not as bad as the small-time lovey-dovey restaurant robbers. But they're not as bad as Vincent, the hit man with a heart of gold (and cultural sensitivity) who kills people. But Vincent is not as bad as Marsellus, the brutal gangland boss who kills people for giving his wife a foot rub. And none of them are as bad as the two kidnapping, torturing sadomasochistic hicks.

In many ways *Pulp Fiction* was one of the first self-consciously postmodern mainstream films, heralding a new way of looking at reality in storytelling. It would soon be followed by a plethora of movies playing with and questioning the difference between reality and fantasy, truth and illusion, fiction and nonfiction, authentic and artificial. This questioning of reality in the movies can be categorized into two ways, both of which we will look at: (1) the *fusion* of reality with fantasy, and (2) the *confusion* of reality with fantasy.[8]

---

[8]I use the term *fantasy* here not in the specific sense of fantasy genre, with its mystical creatures and such, but in the more general sense of creative imagination as opposed to factual events.

The Fusion of Reality with Fantasy

Literature and film have often provided a portal between the two worlds of fantasy and reality, from rabbit holes to wardrobes to time machines. But the modernist approach to storytelling uses fantasy or illusion as a means of expressing the true underlying reality of existence. The action in *Star Wars* may have taken place in a galaxy far, far away, but this movie really tells a tale about good and evil right here in our own world. It took itself seriously as a world unto itself in order to capture and express *our* reality in the metaphorical terms of another world.

The postmodern sensibility, since it doesn't believe in underlying reality, concludes that story cannot be about reality; it can only be about itself. Witness such live action/animation hybrids as *Who Framed Roger Rabbit?* (1988), *Cool World* (1992) and *Monkeybone* (2001), in which the protagonists self-consciously interact with cartoon fantasy worlds that they know and understand to be cartoon fantasy worlds. Others, like *Hook* (1991) and *Jumanji* (1995), use live-action fantasy, but the context is still the same: the intersection and fusion of reality with fantasy.

Self-conscious storytelling is also the basis of the horror franchise *Scream* (1996) and its sequels. Here you have horror movies deliberately describing the conventions of horror movies *within* the movies themselves and then overthrowing some of those conventions or even mocking them. The equally successful horror spoof franchise *Scary Movie* (2000) and its sequel takes it one step further and spoofs the *Scream* franchise— a spoof of a spoof. These are movies that are about movies that are about movies.

Of course, genre spoof movies have been around for a long time, with everything from *Airplane* (1980) to the *Naked Gun* (1988) franchise and many others. But *Scream* marks a move to a more self-referential awareness of their own story by the characters within the story.

In *Scream,* writer Kevin Williamson has his characters talk about classic horror films, like *Nightmare on Elm Street, Halloween* and *Friday the 13th* throughout the entire film, while the same things happen to them. The characters even speak of their own world in terms of its being a horror movie. The heroine, Sidney Prescott is called on the phone by the killer. He asks her why she doesn't watch scary movies. She replies, "Because they're all the same. It's always some stupid killer stalking some big-breasted girl—who can't act—who always runs up the stairs when she should be going out the front door. They're ridiculous." When the killer attacks Sidney in her house, she tries to go out the front door, but it's too well locked, so she is forced to run up the stairs, just like the convention that it is.

Later Sidney tells her boyfriend, "But this is life. This isn't a movie." He responds, "Sure it is, Sid. It's all a movie. Life's one great big movie. Only you can't pick your genre." Near the end of the movie, the group of kids are watching the movie *Halloween,* and one of the teens explains the "rules" of horror as the killer kills more of them in the same way:

 **There are certain rules that one must abide by in order to successfully survive a horror movie. For instance: (1) You can never have sex. The minute you get a little nookie, you're as good as gone. Sex always equals death. (2) Never drink or do drugs. The sin factor. It's an extension of number one. And (3) never, ever, ever, under any circumstances, say, "I'll be right back."**

And of course someone just then says, "I'll be right back"—and he is killed.[9]

The idea of a story within a story is not novel. From the Bible to Shakespeare and other sources, plays within plays have been a helpful dramatic tool to ancients and modernists alike. The difference lies in the postmodernist's intent to focus on the story as a story, and *only* as a story,

---

[9]In the sequel, *Scream 2* (1997), this play on self-reference continues with the added factor of a movie within the movie that was made of the previous movie's "true" murder story. This sort of movie-within-a-movie approach is taken to an extreme in *Urban Legends: Final Cut* (2001), the sequel to *Urban Legends* (1998), which is about a killer who makes scary urban legends of killers come true. In *Final Cut* the heroine is making a film about these very urban legends as her crew is systematically rubbed out one by one in the same ways. The success of these teen-oriented horror spoofs has spawned a similar version in *Not Another Teen Movie* (2001), which is a self-conscious spoof movie about teen genre movies.

not as a means for communicating reality. Remember, for the postmodern, there is no reality for art to communicate, so art is about art, not about something else. An obsession with the shallowness of genre for its own sake is the postmodern hallmark of identity.

Shrek (2001), written by Ted Elliot, Terry Rossio, Joe Stillman and Roger S. H. Schulman, is another example of a self-referential genre movie, in particular, a fairy tale deconstructing fairy tales. It's the story of an ogre named Shrek whose life of angry solitude in the swamp is violated by homeless fairy tale characters who have been dispossessed by the evil Lord Farquaad. In order to get his swamp back, Shrek must go and rescue Princess Fiona from a dark tower guarded by a dragon and bequeath her to Farquaad. He's interested in saving the princess only to save his swamp. On the journey back, the princess openly complains about how this very story is not following the necessary structure of a fairy tale. She is supposed to be rescued by a handsome knight who loves her, not by an ugly ogre who couldn't care less about her. She's also supposed to be a fair, helpless maiden, not the impolite and obnoxious kung fu expert that she is. This kind of banter abounds throughout this anti-fairy tale, as does crude humor and other mocking of traditional fairy tales. In one scene, parodying a famous scene from a Disney movie, Fiona sings a song with a songbird, but she hits a pitch so loud that the bird explodes, and so Fiona cooks the bird's three eggs for breakfast.

The final moral of *Shrek* is also an upending of a traditional fairy tale plot. Fiona is cursed by a spell that changes her beautiful Barbie-doll looks into those of an ogre during the night hours. But the spell will be broken and she will remain as "true love's beauty" permanently when she engages in "love's first kiss." By the end, she and Shrek have fallen for each other and they kiss. But rather than true love's beauty being the Barbie doll, she becomes the ogre permanently—which suits Shrek perfectly!

For all of *Shrek's* anti-fairy tale veneer, it actually communicates some very traditional fairy tale morals: one should marry for true love, not position or power; beauty is in the eye of the beholder; true beauty is the inner person; or as Shrek himself says, "You shouldn't judge people before you know them." This apparent anti-fairy tale turns out to be a traditional fairy tale after all—but with an attitude.

Other Fusions

In the recent example of Skip Wood's *Swordfish* (2001), John Travolta, playing a ruthless criminal, waxes eloquent in an opening monologue about how movies lack realism. He speaks of how movies are more like morality tales in which the bad guys can't win and audiences love happy endings. Then he talks about how *Dog Day Afternoon* would have been a more realistic movie if Al Pacino had started killing hostages one by one until the authorities met his demands. We then discover that Travolta's character is actually talking to some feds in a negotiation because he himself is a bank robber and is about to kill his hostages. Here is another movie engaging in self-reflection about movies.

The fusion of reality and fantasy is given a more literal twist in the movies *The Purple Rose of Cairo* (1985) and *The Last Action Hero* (1993). In Woody Allen's *Purple Rose,* the heroine's pathetic, miserable life with an abusive husband is improved when a dashing, romantic movie hero literally walks out of a movie screen and into her life. The movie explores the differences of the fantasy life we envision in movies and the hard realities we actually experience as the movie character has difficulty getting along in a real world that does not comport with his movie existence.

The *Last Action Hero,* written by Shane Black and David Arnott, is similar in that a young, troubled movie fan gets an enchanted movie ticket that magically transports him into the world of a movie with his action idol (played by Arnold Schwarzenegger as a parody of himself). When the movie bad guy gets a hold of the magic ticket and realizes he can escape into the "real" world, where bad guys really do win, Arnold and the kid have to chase him. But the violence of the real world is not at all like the movies for the action hero. Bullets really kill and punches can break your own fist.

Another result of the fusion of reality and fantasy is the melding of real-life characters into fictional stories. After all, if the two worlds are blurred, then why not blur historical characters with other fictions? *I.Q.* (1994) is a What if? story about Albert Einstein matchmaking for his niece. Academy Award winner *Shakespeare in Love* (1998), by Marc Norman and Tom Stoppard, is a fictitious love story about how Shakespeare came up with *Romeo and Juliet,* written and acted in the style of a Shakespearean romantic comedy. It is a story about a storyteller telling stories.

The dark side of this storytelling genre is *The Player* (1992), Michael Tolkin's black comedy of the insanity of Hollywood. It's a crime drama of a producer killing a screenwriter and taking the credit for his screenplay—and he gets away with it, defying the justice-oriented endings of most Hollywood films. Many movie stars appear in cameos throughout the film as themselves in this blending of fiction and reality. In fact, making a movie about the moviemaking business, with all its sense of shallow unreality, has become a genre in and of itself, hearkening back to the classics *Sunset Boulevard* (1950) and *Day of the Locust* (1975). Witness such films as *The Big Picture* (1989), *Swimming with the Sharks* (1994), *Get Shorty* (1995), *Burn, Hollywood, Burn* (1997), *Bowfinger* (1999), *State and Main* (2000) and others.

A Knight's Tale (2001) is Brian Helgeland's fictional medieval story about jousting, with the historical English poet Geoffrey Chaucer as one of the characters. In this movie, medieval jousting tournaments are staged like modern sports contests, complete with the crowd clapping to the song "We Will Rock You" by the modern band Queen, as well as a royal dance breaking out into modern choreography to a David Bowie song. Here is self-conscious storytelling about stories with no pretense to reality.

Perhaps the epitome of the fusion of fantasy and reality, of the past with the present, of a movie within a movie, is *Moulin Rouge* (2001) by Baz Luhrmann. This musical fantasy reinvents the myth of Orpheus as a turn-of-the-century Bohemian cabaret in Paris. Yet most of its songs are from the likes of Elton John, Madonna, the Police, David Bowie, the Beatles and other late-twentieth-century pop artists.

Historical characters like Henri de Toulouse-Lautrec show up in this fictional paean to indulgence and style, an environment where the aristocracy (fantasy) commingles with the bourgeoisie (reality). It is hyper-paced and fragmented and even has a "play within the play" that recapitulates the same story that is happening to the characters themselves. In the movie an impoverished poet falls for a courtesan in a cabaret that a jealous duke is trying to own for himself. The play that the poet has written and the courtesan is acting in, with the financial support of the duke, is about a Turkish harem woman who falls for a poor writer instead of her rich sultan. And the title of the cabaret play is "Spectacular, Spectacular"—another reflection of the postmodern obsession with spectacle over depth, style over substance, story over reality.

Another, darker version of the self-conscious postmodern musical is *Dancer in the Dark* (2000) by Lars Von Trier. This is the story of an immigrant single mother who is going blind and working at a dreary factory in order to buy her son the surgery he'll need to arrest the same genetically inherited blindness—a metaphor for her spiritual condition.

She comes to America because she thinks it is like the movies with which she is so in love. She lives in denial of her actual baneful existence by acting in a musical play herself and mentally escaping into her musicals. But her life takes a dreadful turn when she is tragically "forced" into killing a neighbor, goes to jail and is ultimately hung for her crime—a true antimusical.

The movie ironically combines musical numbers with such atypical situations as lifeless, dehumanizing factory labor and even the heroine's death by hanging at the prison. And that is the point of the movie: to show that fantasy and reality do not fit together. Life is not like the movies, and we are fools if we hope for it to be. A simpleton character in the movie early on says that he doesn't understand why the heroine loves musicals so much. After all, he muses, he doesn't break out into song in real life. Ironically, later in the movie, he in fact does.

The Confusion of Reality with Fantasy

The fusion of fantasy with reality can be taken a step further into a blurring or confusing of the two to the point where we are not sure which is which or whether there is a difference at all. If *Pulp Fiction* opened the doorway to the use of nonlinear reality in popular movies, then two movies, *The Sixth Sense* and *The Matrix,* both released in 1999, mark the next step into the *confusion* of reality with fantasy.

In M. Night Shyamalan's *The Sixth Sense,* the main character, Malcolm (a child psychologist played by Bruce Willis), discovers that his own sense of reality is the exact opposite of what it really is. And there is no greater confusion than to think you are alive when in fact you are dead. [10] Malcolm is haunted by his own past failure to help a child client find healing, so he haunts the world of a psychically gifted child, Cole (played by Haley Joel Osment), with the same problem as Malcolm's previous client. This attempt on Malcolm's part to help Cole is his desire to atone for his past mistake. After Malcolm effectively enables Cole to accept himself and his strange gifts as valuable (embodied in Cole's acting as young King Arthur in a school play), only then can Malcolm find his own redemption or peace of mind. Malcolm becomes aware of his blindness to reality, is freed from his restless walking of the earth as an unaware ghost and is then able to disappear into movie heaven. In other words, Malcolm is redeemed by redeeming another.

The Matrix and other sci-fi movies take this same reality blindness to a technological extreme. The genre of science fiction seems well suited for the postmodern fusion/confusion of reality. Steven Connor writes in *Postmodern Culture,* "Science fiction is a particularly intriguing case for postmodernist theory, precisely because the genre of science fiction

---

[10]*The Others* (2001), by writer-director Alejandro Amenábar, and starring Nicole Kidman, follows *The Sixth Sense* in this same theme, but within the context of a haunted house. In fact, many "ghost stories" are not so much about scaring live people as they are about departed souls finding redemption or satisfaction in completing unfinished business, like justice for unsolved crimes. This could aptly be likened to the biblical notion of blood crying out from the ground for vengeance (Genesis 4:10). Examples of this redemption theme include *Ghost* (1990), *Stir of Echoes* (1999) and *The Haunting* (1999).

belongs, chronologically at least, to the period of modernism's emergence. . . . Modernism experimented with ways of seeing and saying the
real; science fiction experimented realistically with forms of reality
themselves."[11]

Science fiction seems to be able to express the postmodern sensibilities of alternate realities with particular effectiveness. With the preva-
lence of the Copenhagen interpretation of quantum theory in the
scientific world, these sensibilities have been brought to the forefront in
sci-fi storytelling. The Copenhagen school, the dominant voice in quantum physics, has drawn a relativistic philosophy of reality from the
Heisenberg uncertainty principle. The uncertainty principle concludes
that it is impossible for us to measure with complete accuracy the simul-
taneous position and speed of atomic particles. From this impossibility of
perfect physical measurements was derived the "drastic philosophy" (as
historian of science Stanley Jaki put it) of the impossibility of discerning
between being and nonbeing.[12] This leap of faith from epistemology (our

---

[11]Steven Connor, *Postmodernist Culture: An Introduction to Theories of the Contemporary*
(Cambridge, Mass.: Blackwell, 1997), p. 134.

[12]Stanley L. Jaki, *Chance or Reality and Other Essays* (Lanham, Md.: University Press of
America, 1986), p. 14. The uncertainty principle is quoted in Joel and Ethan Coen's movie *The
Man Who Wasn't There* (2001) by a lawyer as a means of casting doubt on the guilt of a man
being tried for murder. The title itself refers to the protagonist, Ed Crane (played by Billy Bob
Thornton), who calls himself a "ghost"—someone who is so nondescript, so underwhelming,
that people don't even notice his presence. It's like he's not there. At first Ed's wife is put on
trial for the murder of her boss—a murder that was actually committed by Ed (although in
self-defense). Ed confesses to his wife's lawyer that *he* is the one guilty of the murder, but the
lawyer dismisses this confession as an unacceptable story to protect the accused. He never
bothers to consider that Ed is actually telling the truth, because he is not interested in the truth,
just in a believable *story.* Because Ed "isn't there" in people's minds, they all concoct outrageous scenarios to explain the murder (from alien abduction to a jealous lover). None of them
even considers the true facts of the matter, which the audience has the privilege of knowing.
Ed's innocent wife goes to jail for the crime she did not commit. Later Ed is put on trial for a
different murder that he did not commit. In Ed's new trial the same attorney comes back to
defend him. He explains to the jury that, according to the uncertainty principle, the act of looking at something changes the object of perception, therefore hindering the juror's ability to see
the facts impartially. "The more you look, the less you know." Because the jurors need to conclude beyond a reasonable doubt, modern humanity's dilemma of the inability to "know" facts
hinders their ability to convict anyone of anything. He points at Ed and explains that he is the

theory of knowledge) to ontology (reality itself) opened up a Pandora's box of theories for the sci-fi genre to exploit with abandon, from the many-worlds theory to the cyberpunk virtual confusion of reality itself.

Blade Runner (1982) was the cult classic that first gave us a postmodern questioning of the real and the artificial. Its hero, Deckard, is a bounty hunter tracing renegade androids who are virtually indistinguishable from real humans, only to discover in the end that he himself might be an android. This revelation remains deliberately ambiguous by the storytellers (less so in the director's cut) in order to leave us wondering and debating about it for years to come. Most books discussing postmodernism have used *Blade Runner* as their example of postmodern filmmaking in all its detail, so we will move on to more recent films.

The Matrix, The Thirteenth Floor (1999) and *eXistenZ* (1999) have all extended the *Blade Runner* real/artificial motif into a new horizon: virtual reality. The dawning of a new millennium of virtual reality in computers has brought a new vision of humanity and its future. And that new vision is a postmodern one through and through. What these movies do is establish a virtual reality made through computers that is so real that the characters do not know the difference between the virtual world and their real world—one of the philosophical corollaries to the postmodern notion that there is no "text," no ultimate underlying reality. If all we have are our own cultural prejudices, by which we

 **Director's Cut**

For a brain-stretching postmodern analysis of *Blade Runner,* see Gary Bush, "Blade Runner (Director's Cut) and the Semantics of Semiotic Collapse" (master's thesis, University of California, Irvine), available at ‹www.godawa.com›, along with further reading on quantum physics.

---

embodiment of "modern man." Actually, the camera shot has the lawyer pointing directly into the camera at *us,* the audience, in an obvious implication of our own experience of the problem. I think the movie is making fun of the absurd ramifications of the postmodern loss of identity of the individual person. By negating Ed's personal identity, the characters lose their ability to see the plain truth right in front of their eyes. These kinds of metaphysical musings are a staple of most Coen brothers' films.

construct the world around us, then in fact we exist in a continuum of infinite "realities," all relative to the individual and his or her interpretation. The world is a virtual playground.

The Matrix has reshaped the sci-fi genre for the new millennium. Its hero, Neo, keeps a secret computer disk in the chapter "On Nihilism" of an actual, well-known postmodern book, *Simulacra and Simulation.* The word *simulacrum* is defined by David Harvey as "a state of such near perfect replication that the difference between the original and the copy becomes almost impossible to spot."[13] In like manner Neo soon discovers that what we all think is the real world is actually a virtual world created by computers that have conquered the human race and turned people into energy sources to run the computers. We are literally having the life sucked out of us and have been given the illusion of the matrix so that we do not wake up to our slavery.

This syncretistic film mixes the Christian idea of spiritual rebirth with the Neo-Platonic notion that enlightenment is found in our "waking up" from our ignorance. What we think is reality is actually a dream state that blinds us to the true state of humanity. Morpheus, the person appointed to find "the One" who will free us from the illusion of the matrix, echoes the essence of this theme of questioning reality when he asks the as-yet-unenlightened Neo:

 Have you ever had a dream, Neo, that you were so sure was real? What if you were unable to wake from that dream? How would you know the difference between the dream world and the real world?

Ironically, though the film plays with Eastern concepts of physical reality being a projection of mind ("there is no spoon"), the story still necessitates a real world that opposes the illusion. And this real world, which is not a creation of the mind, is bound by harsh reality, laws of nature, right and wrong. This real world is not even as enjoyable as the

---

[13]David Harvey, *The Condition of Postmodernity: An Enquiry into the Origins of Cultural Change* (Cambridge, Mass.: Blackwell, 1995), p. 289.

illusory world. The "enlightened" guys eat goop for food, dress in rags and fly around in a ravished, postapocalyptic environment without any sunlight. But it's clear that this dark reality is preferable to a fantasy illusion that makes us happy. Why? Because it's the truth—it's *reality*. And reality is ultimately preferable to dreams or illusions, even if it is harsh and depressing.[14]

In *eXistenZ* (the German word for "existence" used by the existential philosopher Martin Heidegger as the "being thereness" of humanity)[15] the heroes play a deadly virtual reality game, only to discover at the end that what they thought was the real world was simply a continuation of the virtual world from which they were coming. A character asks the last line of the film, "Are we still in the game?" and we fade to black. We cannot know illusion from reality.

Not all movies that deal with the illusion/reality game are sci-fi. It has become a creative technique explored successfully in such films as *The Usual Suspects* (1995), in which the narrator telling the story of a criminal heist turns out to have fooled the police and audience about his own innocence. The narrator turns out to be the true criminal, and by the time he gets away, we learn that the entire movie we've just seen has been his deceptive storytelling—and we bought it. This film thus offers a postmodern challenge to how easily we are deceived about what we think is reality.

The technique of filming characters' lies as if they were truth has been used in many films, like *Gossip* (2000), *The Tailor of Panama* (2001), *The Game* (1997), *Under Suspicion* (2000) and *Mulholland Drive* (2001). In *Under Suspicion* an effective police detective (played by Morgan Freeman) is so immersed in psychological analysis that he brings a wealthy man (played by Gene Hackman) to a tearful confession of a

---

[14]The independent film *Waking Life* (2001) by Richard Linklater is a postmodern polemic of a character who wakes up from dreams into other dreams and can never seem to find his way to "reality," all the while listening to a litany of individuals espouse their personal existential, postmodern and evolutionary philosophies.

[15]Walter Kaufmann, *Existentialism from Dostoevsky to Sartre* (Cleveland: World, 1970), p. 213.

child murder through sheer verbal coercion. We even see the murder replayed through Hackman's viewpoint. The only problem is, Hackman is ultimately proven innocent of the crime, thereby illustrating the power of suggestion upon our memories and understanding of facts and reality.

Fight Club. Another film that uses the inability to distinguish between illusion and reality is *Fight Club* (1999), starring Brad Pitt and Edward Norton. In this deeply disturbing film adapted by Jim Uhls from the novel by Chuck Palahniuk, the main character, a nameless "Jack," struggles through an angst-ridden, white-collar, consumer lifestyle. He sees the emptiness of this experience and falls into faking terminal diseases so he can go to support groups and connect with those who are facing death and sloughing off the facades of life. For him, encountering death is a means of finding life.

But these vicarious encounters with mortality soon prove ineffective, and Jack meets Tyler Durden, a wild and crazy anarchist who starts a "fight club" with Jack where men can break through their meaningless existence via the shock of pain experienced in their fights. This is a creed of existentialism: authentic existence is discovered through encounters with pain and death that emphasize the urgency of living.[16] Or as the philosopher Heidegger would have it, "My own personal history is authentically meaningful when I accept responsibility for my own existence, seize my own future possibilities and live in enduring awareness of my own future death."[17]

There is much truth to the axiom that consumer culture kills the spirit. It is indeed a horrible reality that in our culture we anesthetize ourselves into spiritual numbness by our pursuit of the next material good that will please us, by finding a rut that we can become comfortable with and so never have to face our meaningless existence without God. As Tyler says with proverbial slogans that ring so true,

---

[16]Peter Koestenbaum, "Jaspers, Karl," in *The Encyclopedia of Philosophy,* ed. Paul Edwards (New York: Macmillan, 1972), p. 256.

[17]Quoted in Terry Eagleton, *Literary Theory: An Introduction* (Minneapolis: University of Minnesota Press, 1983), p. 65.

You are not your bank account. . . . You are not the clothes that you wear. . . . You are not the car that you drive. . . . You are not your grande latte. . . . You have to give up. . . . You have to realize that someday, you will die. . . . Until you know that, you are useless. . . . Only after disaster can we be resurrected. . . . Everything is falling apart. . . . This is your life—and it's ending one minute at a time.

Jack and many others eventually follow Tyler to the point of messianic cult worship. "In Tyler we trust." Their violence increases toward others as they embark on a spree of vandalizing private property that reaches its climax in the planned destruction of the ultimate symbols of consumer bondage: the buildings of credit card companies. This nihilistic annihilation of values rings with the sound of Nietzsche's Overman creating the self through destruction:

> The "desirability" of the mediocre is what we others combat . . . the highest man . . . would be the man who represented the antithetical character of existence most strongly, as its glory and sole justification—Commonplace men can represent only a tiny nook and corner of this natural character: they perish when the multiplicity of elements and the tension of opposites increases. . . . That man must grow better *and* more evil is my formula for this inevitability.[18]

It is here that Jack finally has a divine epiphany, or more accurately, a diabolical bombshell, when he comes face to face with the fact that Tyler is his own suppressed alter ego that is leading him to self-destruction. Tyler was a creation of Jack's own mind. Now Jack must liberate himself from his unregenerate dark side if he is to find redemption. This theme of self-delusion and the depraved side of humanity is reminiscent of the classic Robert Louis Stevenson tale *Dr. Jekyll and Mr. Hyde*.

Memento. A movie that questions our epistemic search for truth and our inimitable propensity to self-deception is the low-budget independent

---

[18]Friedrich Nietzsche, *The Will To Power,* ed. Walter Kaufmann (New York: Vintage, 1968), p. 470.

sleeper hit *Memento* (2001), written and directed by Christopher Nolan. This mystery thriller's central premise is about an insurance claims investigator named Leonard (Guy Pearce) who is seeking the man who raped and killed his wife. When he finds him, he will kill him. His problem is that he was himself cranially wounded in the attack and has lost his short-term memory in the process. He forgets everyone he now meets as well as everything that occurs in his life after the attack. Consequently, he can trust no one and must constantly rediscover what he is doing and who he meets every few hours or so. He ends up tattooing the most important things he must remember onto his body and takes Polaroid photographs of people, places and things in order to jot down important notes to himself.

The gimmick of this film is that it uses postmodern nonlinear storytelling. It tells the story in reverse! So we begin with Leonard shooting the alleged killer and then discover with the hero his past as we progress backward toward the beginning. This technique of reversing the entire story helps us experience the hero's lack of memory of his own experiences.

All along the way, we don't really know who he can trust and who is deceiving him. And as we get to the end of the story, which is actually the beginning, we learn that he killed the wrong man, because in the midst of a heated dispute with the very guy who was helping him, he jotted down notes against him that weren't true. He vents his anger in a fit of rage, and because he trusts only what he has written (but can never remember that he deliberately wrote it wrong), he ends up killing the wrong man.

But that's only half of it. *Everyone* in the movie ends up using our hero in one way or another. And his own self-deception is highlighted by the fact that because of his memory loss, he ends up forgetting that he was the one who accidentally killed his wife! She was not killed in the attack; she was a diabetic, and he killed her by accidentally giving her an overdose of insulin. He "remembers" this story as someone else's story in order to alleviate his guilt.

Memento carries the astute insight that we are self-deceiving creatures by nature who are easily deceived by our own whims and are therefore unworthy of the faith we place in ourselves. If our epistemic starting point, our standard of truth and knowledge, is itself flawed, then our beliefs about the world are flawed and will lead to false conclusions and bad decisions. In other words, the starting point that we place our faith in had better be correct to begin with or we're in trouble. And it had better not be ourselves, because we are the source of our own problems. As Leonard repeats to himself in the movie, "We lie to ourselves to make us happy."[19]

At the end of *Memento* Leonard tells himself, "I have to believe in a world outside my own mind. I have to believe that my actions still have meaning . . . even if I can't remember them. I have to believe that when my eyes are closed, the world's still there." Leonard here makes an irrational leap of faith in an objective world he cannot prove (due to his lack of memory) in order to live with meaning rather than absurdity.

Other Confusions

The Blair Witch Project (1999), an extremely low-budget box office hit written and directed by Daniel Myrick and Eduardo Sánchez, is another example of the postmodern illusion/reality confusion. It's a story of some young adults who go off into the woods of Burkittesville, Maryland, to make a documentary of the legend of the Blair witch—a tradition that seems to surround multiple murders throughout the local history. The moral of this parable of our fascination with evil is that without a moral compass to guide us, we will be overcome by the very evil that we seek to understand.

The kids get lost in the woods without a compass and are eventually overtaken by the killer behind the legend. The groundbreaking uniqueness of this story is its fabrication as a true documentary of the film footage discovered in the woods several years after the students went

---

[19]Another film that embodies this lying to ourselves is *Mulholland Drive* (2001) by David Lynch. It's the story of a naive Midwestern girl just arrived in California to be in the movies. She saves another, older actress and falls in love with her as a conniving director steals the older actress away from her. Near the end, the entire story of characters is revealed to be the mental construct of the newly arriving actress, who is actually a jealous, psychotic lesbian imagining herself as the pure, innocent heroine and everyone else who blocks her goals as devious or manipulated weaklings. The power of self-deception runs deep in human nature. We all see ourselves as heroes of our own stories—often at the expense of the truth.

missing. This pseudodocumentary, "real TV" approach brought a new depth to the scariness of horror movies because of its pretended realism.

Even the *Blair Witch* website, which was hugely successful, was designed to appear like a true reporter's presentation of historical facts and evidence surrounding the event and its history. And most disturbing of all, this blurring of fantasy and reality was so successful that many young people actually believed it *was* a true story—a rather macabre revelation of the gullibility of the "pomo generation," children who will believe falsehoods simply because they saw it in the media.

Passion of Mind (2000), starring Demi Moore, is the story of a woman who seems to be living in two realities: one as an author in France and the other as an editor for a major book publisher in New York. Her predicament is to discover which life is real and which is the dream. She ultimately does figure it out, and this points to a particular dilemma of the illusion/reality challenge of postmodern movies. No matter how strongly the point is made that we are self-deceived and cannot trust our understanding of what is objectively real, the characters must always do so within the context of an *objective* reality from which to illumine this self-delusion.

Sliding Doors (1998) is an example of the many-worlds idea as well as the "butterfly effect" of chaos theory, which states that little changes in a system can result in dramatic ramifications on other interacting systems (e.g., small differences in weather patterns create widely divergent results). Gwyneth Paltrow stars as a woman whose life we see split into two lives that run parallel, with the mere difference of catching a train or not. In the one life, she *doesn't* catch the train and is therefore not home in time to catch her boyfriend in bed with another woman, keeping her life the same in its self-deception. In the other life, she catches the train on time and catches her boyfriend, and so her life takes a completely different turn. The movie intercuts between these "lives" of one person as they each head toward widely different conclusions.[20]

---

[20]The Jet Li action film *The One* (2001) has characters interacting with 124 different parallel universes.

One of the most recent cinematic expressions of the postmodern illusion/reality confusion is *Final Fantasy: The Spirits Within* (2001). Based on a video game, this film is the most lifelike animation yet created. Every attempt was made with state-of-the-art software to create human characters that did not look like animated cartoons but like real flesh-and-blood actors. The stated goal of many computer animation studios is to ultimately achieve a style of animation that is so real that the audience will not know the difference. They will create virtual human characters that appear to exist but are actually manufactured illusions.

A Beautiful Mind (2001) is an exploration of the confusion of fantasy and reality. Genius mathematician John Nash suffers from schizophrenia and imagines several people into his life—people who lead him into paranoid delusionary behaviors. He doesn't believe that these people are hallucinations until he realizes that they haven't aged after many years. The drugs prescribed to fight his schizophrenia impede his mathematical abilities, so he decides to face his delusions without medication. With the help of his wife he gains victory over his mental dysfunctions; the hallucinations don't go away but recede into the background.

Vanilla Sky (2001) stars Tom Cruise as a playboy whose disfigurement in a car crash forces him to reconsider what is most important in life. He arranges to be cryonically frozen until his maladies can be fixed, and opts for supplemental "Lucid Dreams" while he waits for his awakening. A computer glitch erases his memory and makes his dreams seem all the more real, and he comes to realize that even a hard life is preferable to a fantasy.

Concluding Nonscientific Postscript

The proposition that we cannot trust ourselves or our traditional forms of knowledge (epistemology) as an ultimate standard of truth leaves the postmodernist in a quandary. While some feign contentment with an "absolute" relativism of truth in a universe of so-called chance and randomness, the reflective skeptic will conclude that relativism is a self-refuting absolute truth claim. If relativism were absolutely and universally true, it would be false because relativism denies absolute and universal truth by definition. So in order for relativism to be true, it would have to be false: reductio ad absurdum (reduction to absurdity).

Furthermore, we could not know that our perceptions of reality were in fact illusions unless we could point to an objective absolute standard of real versus illusory perceptions. The claim of illusion presupposes a knowledge of reality against which illusion is shown to be illusion; otherwise, you simply cannot know it is illusion. Rather than concluding that all is illusion and that we have no knowledge of reality, the honest skeptic will ask, "How do I know which ultimate standard of reality is true?"

A positive heritage of postmodernism is the questioning of our *views* of reality, rather than questioning reality *itself.* Postmodern analysis brings a long overdue exposé of many false assumptions inherent in our modern Enlightenment way of thinking. And many of the movies we have examined in this chapter do just that. While questioning our notions of reality, they do not deny reality altogether. And this makes them postmodern in a positive sense, not necessarily in a negative sense. Not all postmodern tactics are fallacious. As Veith points out, there is a difference between being postmodern in our relevancy and being a postmodern*ist.*[21] The postmodern questions our notions of reality, and this is wise, but postmodern*ism* denies reality itself, which is self-refuting.

Much of our society's conception of reality *is* wrong and in need of challenging. If we understand the context of our time and culture, we will better interpret the broader social implications of many movies beyond our personal appreciation. The illusion/reality dilemma is a great storytelling tool to challenge our assumptions about reality and truth, but taken to its extreme (that of denying *all* reality), it suffers under the weight of its own contradiction.

---

[21]Veith, *Postmodern Times,* pp. xii-xiii, 221-23.

Watch and Learn

1. Watch *The Last Action Hero* or *The Purple Rose of Cairo*. What is being professed about the nature of reality and fantasy and how they affect each other? Refer to specific scenes and dialogue in the movie that reinforce your point. What claims are made about indulging in fantasy? What is the movie arguing about the proper place for fantasy entertainment in our lives? In what ways do you agree and disagree?

2. Watch *The Matrix*. Which world is better: the real one or the computer-generated one? Why? Examine the argument made by Cypher, the character who betrays Neo. In what ways does his attitude reflect those of actual people in our contemporary world? How does the movie reflect your own worldview on how people are deceived about reality?

 **5** **Other Worldviews**

Although existentialism and postmodernism are influential viewpoints in many movies today, they are not the only ones. In this chapter I would like to offer a brief survey of worldviews that have played at a theater near you. Space limitations forbid addressing them all, so I have chosen several that I consider important to discuss. Let's take a look at fate, monism, emergent evolution and neopaganism in the movies.

Fate in the Movies

When storytellers don't want to admit their Creator into their worldview, and yet don't want to face the horror and meaninglessness of the random universe they are left with, they substitute fate for the living God. The benefit of this tactic is that it gives the storyteller all the benefits of a personal loving God, complete with a happy ending, but none of the moral accountability. As C. S. Lewis eloquently stated:

When you are feeling fit and the sun is shining and you do not want to believe that the whole universe is a mere mechanical dance of atoms, it is nice to be able to think of this great mysterious Force rolling on through the centuries and carrying you on its crest. If, on the other hand, you want to do something rather shabby, the Life-Force, being only a blind force, with no morals and no mind, will never interfere with you like that troublesome God.[1]

Cast Away (2001), written by William Broyles Jr., is an example of fate as a God substitute. It's a thought-provoking story of a FedEx employee named Chuck Noland (played by Tom Hanks), whose life is dictated by his time schedule and whose plane crashes in the ocean, resulting in him washing up on a deserted island. The entire middle of the film is a contemplative series of scenes of a man facing his helpless solitude—a good examination of how so many things we consider important fall away when we lose the conveniences and distractions of modern life. We have allowed ourselves to become tyrannized by time and therefore miss out on what's really important all around us.

This survivor relives the so-called evolutionary "stages of humankind" as he learns to find shelter, create tools, build fire and ultimately seek companionship. God is conspicuously absent from the entire search, unlike its classic literary predecessor, *Robinson Crusoe*. Not once does this shipwrecked victim ever consider his Creator, even to lash out at him for his predicament. He is all alone in a naturalistic universe.

There are a few spiritual symbols that are secularized into subtle metaphors for his "quest." A set of wings (angel?) on a FedEx package become Chuck's sailboat symbol. He uses his own blood to make a face on his volleyball friend, Mr. Wilson ("bone of my bone, flesh of my flesh"?). And after Chuck sets out to sea to find civilization, he encounters a whale at night that stares at him (but this is more an expression of the unity with nature that he has achieved than it is a deliberate reference to the biblical Jonah).

At the end of the film, Chuck finds his way back to civilization. The

---

[1]C. S. Lewis, *Mere Christianity* (New York: Macmillan, 1960), p. 35.

woman whose "angel wings" mail package washed up on shore and kept him going in his darkest hour just happens to be a beautiful and available woman for our lonely returned hero—a substitute for the woman he had lost. So humanity finds meaning in hope for another human being, and the benevolent impersonal fate will work it all out for us in the end.

Another example of a secularized version of fate devoid of deity can be found in the movie *Serendipity* (2001), written by Marc Klein. It's the story of two individuals (played by John Cusack and Kate Beckinsale) whose lives are magically drawn together into a romantic connection by multiple fortuitous occurrences, as the title itself suggests. Throughout the story, the characters struggle with faith in destiny and personal choices, flipping back and forth between the view that "life's a mess, chaos personified," and "life is a tapestry of events," that "life is a plan."

There is no mention of God in this story, yet the characters interact with the idea of fate as if it were a person who has a wonderful plan for their lives. Like Gideon and his fleece, they seek for "signs" and tempt fate with impossible odds. And at the end of the day, the ultimate purpose of this humanistic impersonal fate is the romanticized love relationship between people.

A negative version of fate can be found in David Webb Peoples's *Twelve Monkeys* (1995). This time-travel picture is crafted like a Greek tragedy of fate on the level of *Oedipus*. The hero, in trying to save the world from biological warfare, is trapped in the never-ending time loop of seeing himself as a child observing his own death as an adult failing to save the world (echoes of Nietzsche's "eternal recurrence"[2]).

The metaphysical notion of eternal recurrence fits well with the scientific theory of an oscillating universe, which posits that the universe is not merely expanding from the Big Bang but is eventually going to stop and

---

[2]Friedrich Nietzsche, "Thus Spoke Zarathustra," in *The Portable Nietzsche,* ed. Walter Kaufmann (New York: Penguin, 1982), pp. 332-33, 341; and *The Gay Science: With a Prelude in Rhymes and an Appendix of Songs,* ed. Walter Kaufmann (New York: Random House, 1974), pp. 273-74. Friedrich Nietzsche's idea of the eternal recurrence or eternal return was another logical result of the "death of God" philosophy. He understood that linear history, with its beginning, middle and end, reflected a Christian worldview of origins and purpose, so he tried

fall inward into a Big Crunch—over and over again, like a bouncing ball, from Big Bang to Big Crunch to Big Bang and back again. This eternal recurrence of an oscillating universe is exactly what Prot, the self-proclaimed alien played by Kevin Spacey in the movie *K-PAX* (2001), alludes to at the end of that story. He explains to Dr. Powell, his psychiatrist (played by Jeff Bridges), this very oscillating universe scenario and how everyone will experience the same life over and over again. His

 **Director's Cut**

Visit ‹www.godawa.com› for further reading on Friedrich Nietzsche.

point is that we had better fix our life, because it's the only one we've got. *K-PAX* exemplifies pop nihilism in the movies.

Nitty-Gritty Fate Films

Pulp Fiction, discussed in an earlier chapter, is not a "fate" film, because it actually addresses the idea of God using miracles to bring redemption into a criminal's life. But it spawned a whole subgenre of films after its own image that *would* embrace fate rather than God within a quirky postmodern context of criminal chic.

One of the redeeming features of *Pulp Fiction*'s celebration of underworld depravity is its wrestling with God. Samuel L. Jackson's hit man character, Jules, recognizes the "touch of God" when he and fellow killer Vincent are miraculously unscathed by a surprise gun attack. All five bullets of a revolver shot at them at point-blank range completely miss them.

Jules argues with the skeptical Vincent that God stopped the bullets by divine intervention. Jules says to his compadre in crime, "What happened here was a miracle, and I want you to acknowledge it." Vincent refuses to do so, thinking he merely witnessed a "freak occurrence." But Jules

---

to replace that linearity with a cyclical view he called eternal recurrence. This view posited that the universe, being eternal, had no beginning but was eternally changing. Since the universe is finite, it will ultimately keep changing through every possible change, recycling all possible states, over and over, throughout all eternity. There is no heaven, no eternal reward and punishment; there is simply the eternal return of everything. A. J. Hoover, *Friedrich Nietzsche: His Life and Thought* (Westport, Conn.: Praeger, 1994), pp. 174-83.

knows better and decides that his killing days are over. He is going to quit "the business" and walk the earth "like Caine in *Kung Fu,* till God puts me where he wants me to be."

Before Jules would kill his victims, he would quote an amalgamation of Bible verses in cold-blooded mockery:

The path of the righteous man is beset on all sides by the inequities of the selfish and the tyranny of evil men. Blessed is he who, in the name of charity and goodwill, shepherds the weak through the valley of darkness, for he is truly his brother's keeper and the finder of lost children. And I will strike down upon thee with great vengeance and furious anger those who would attempt to poison and destroy my brothers. And you will know my name is the Lord when I lay my vengeance upon thee.

But when Jules has his newfound revelation, the true meaning of those verses comes alive to him. He repents of his own "tyranny of evil" and becomes a man of grace, a shepherd to help the weak.

Contrarily, Vincent, who refuses to see the handwriting on the wall, continues on living by the gun and therefore dies by the gun—at the hands of his enemy. These contrasted destinies are rather profound expressions of a biblical truth:

> They shall eat of the fruit of their own way,
> And be satiated with their own devices.
> For the waywardness of the naive will kill them,
> And the complacency of fools will destroy them.
> But he who listens to me shall live securely
> And will be at ease from the dread of evil. . . .
> You will walk in the way of good men
> And keep to the paths of the righteous.
> For the upright will live in the land
> And the blameless will remain in it;
> But the wicked will be cut off from the land. (Proverbs 1:31-33; 2:20-22)

Of course there are a lot of bad guys who *do* get away with murder and robbery in *Pulp Fiction,* but consistency is not a high priority in postmodern morality.

Because of the success of *Pulp Fiction,* there is a new subgenre of films on the rise that I call "nitty-gritty fate films," based on the *Pulp Fiction* paradigm. They are often "smaller," independent films that contain multiple story lines of different people who are mostly lowlife or criminal elements of society and who are unconnected to each other, but through some wild, complex twists of fate end up intersecting all in one moment or day in such a way that all their stories are resolved together.

Some of these nitty-gritty fate films include *Short Cuts* (1993), *2 Days in the Valley* (1996), *Lock, Stock and Two Smoking Barrels* (1998), *Payback* (1999), *Go* (1999), *Small-Time Crooks* (2000), *The Mexican* (2001), *One Night at McCool's* (2001), *The Score* (2001), *Sexy Beast* (2001), *Snatch* (2001) and others. The main characters in these stories are usually small-time criminals who are portrayed as making bad choices rather than as being bad people. By the end of the story, the trouble that these misdirected souls have gotten into is resolved perfectly, and most of the *really* bad guys are punished—and all of this because of the intricate workings of an impersonal fate.

Like *Pulp Fiction* and *Magnolia,* these fate films have the same kind of perfect foreordination of every little event working toward a final purpose, but altogether without God. They often use the postmodern storytelling device of showing nuances of difference between each person's perception of events, and their gritty use of humor and vice turn them into crime spoofs. Let's take a look at some of these nitty-gritty fate films to illustrate the point.

Lock, Stock and Two Smoking Barrels from British writer/director Guy Ritchie takes four different stories and weaves them together into one karmic blend. Four wide-eyed young Cockney card-playing lads of London want to join an illegal, high-rolling card game. The leader of that little game is a gangland boss who is in search of two antique shotguns that have been stolen. A drug lord is growing pot in a house that is about to be raided by some robbers, who just happen to live next door to our four young lads.

When the card players get in life-threatening debt over the rigged card game, they try to make up the money by stealing the drug robbery job away from their next-door neighbors. So the gangland boss sends a killer to take out the kids, the druggies are after the kids to get back their stash, and the intended robbers are after the kids to regain their dignity.

All their plans go awry and all the bad guys descend upon each other unwittingly in one huge gun battle in which they all die, leaving the young kids alive and debt-free. It's a perfect circle: the bad guys kill each other; big crimes may not pay, but small ones do; and it all works out for "the good" in the end.

Ritchie's rowdy *Snatch* carries on this tradition with a whole new set of crazy characters from different sides of the tracks who also wind up as pawns in some huge web of fate in which divergent lives converge with karmic predestination, the big bad guys kill each other and the good-hearted crooks get away.

2 Days in the Valley, by John Herzfeld, is another fate-works-it-all-out story. Herzfeld sets up a plethora of divergent, unconnected lives that all come together with magnetic ferocity in two days in the San Fernando Valley of southern California. The list of personal stories is of the kind that only a god could keep track of and still end up fixing it all. But fix it all fate does indeed.

The people fate has to fix include a vengeful athlete trying to kill her adulterating husband, a washed-up hit man with a heart of gold, a has-been TV director on the verge of suicide, two bickering cops trying to bust a massage parlor for prostitution, a self-obsessed art dealer with kidney stones and his shy female assistant, and a heartless assassin obsessed with time and jealousy for his blonde, bimbo partner. The assassin and his bimbo get killed. The director falls in love with a tender, loving nurse. The nice-guy hit man falls in love with the shy assistant. And the athlete gets away with murdering her husband.

Monism in the Movies

As indicated earlier, monism is an Eastern worldview that is becoming more fashionable in the West. Monism is the belief that all of reality is ultimately one and that distinctions among things are mere illusion *(maya)*. When I look at a tree or at you, the fact that I see the other as separate from me is an illusion, because ultimately I am one with the tree and with thee.

Humanity's problem is therefore ignorance. The reason why we act wickedly is that we do not know that we are one with all things. If people could only experience oneness with that which they see as separate, they would find peace. This is why monists say that all the different religions are merely masks for the same God. This pantheistic enlightenment is the redemption that is boldly evangelized in two mainstream movies with similar premises: *Powder* (1995) and *Phenomenon* (1996).

Powder, written and directed by Victor Salva, is the story of an *E.T.*-like rejected messiah. Nicknamed "Powder" for his albino skin, he is a young man who is discovered to have the "greatest intellect in the history of mankind" and who is rejected by everyone for his "differentness." A lightning accident before his birth is the cause of his electromagnetic power and his ability to use a higher percentage of his brain than the rest of us.

In a similar spirit, *Phenomenon,* written by Gerald Di Pego, is the story of simple, small-town mechanic, George Malley (played by John Travolta), who also is struck by a mystical bolt of light from the sky. After he picks himself up off the ground, his mind starts to expand and accelerate in intelligence, which results in alienating him from his neighbors.

The redemption communicated by these films is twofold. First, their themes contain the postulate of the Enlightenment: salvation comes through reason. Both George and Powder are portrayed as thoroughly evolved men, superior in intelligence and highly sensitive to the human condition.

After George is hit by his mystical lightning, he is able to master overnight the Spanish he had been having a difficult time learning. He then goes on to learn Portuguese in twenty minutes. He reads three books a night every night, comprehending the mysteries of photovoltaics and quantum physics. He starts to invent things that will solve people's technological problems, like more efficient solar panel technology and a car that can get ninety miles to a gallon of manure. His mind is so energized that he cannot sleep, and he even develops telekinetic abilities to move small objects with the power of his mind.

Powder also retains everything he reads with photographic memory and blows away the I.Q. tests. And yet he is quintessentially a Christlike lover of all life, be it a deer in the woods or a rebellious, hateful reform-school kid.

George is also a Christ figure. Because people cannot understand his newly acquired powers, they become afraid of him, thinking he was touched by aliens. But not the woman he has fallen in love with—or her children. George soon discovers the real reason for his increased brain power: a tumor has buried its roots deep into his brain, and in a strange twist of fate, instead of attacking his brain, it has energized it to its height of genius.

But the tumor finally runs its course and begins to kill George. The kids are sad to see him dying and think they will miss him, but he gives them a humanist "last supper" by telling them to bite into an apple because, when we eat an apple, "it becomes part of us, and we can take it with us forever." Meanwhile, the song "Have a Little Faith in Me" plays over the visuals of the kids taking bites in remembrance of George.

The movie ends with a "resurrection" scene of a huge, once-unfruitful field, now ripe with a harvest of corn because of George's advice. We are witnesses to a secular miracle of rebirth, the dying and rising of a corn god. And we see, one year later, the whole town joyfully celebrating George's birthday with newfound community and happiness—a secularized version of church fellowship.

Powder and *Phenomenon* both conclude that if we only used more of our minds, then we would see our interconnectedness with all things and act more wisely. Knowledge and education breed virtue. George and Powder are examples of the human potential, the possibility of what everyone can be, if we only used our heads more.

Second, both movies offer a Western, bastardized version of monism. In *Powder* the predator deputy sheriff stops hunting and throws out all his guns after Powder "connects" him with the dying deer the deputy had previously shot. The sheriff finds his redemption when Powder is able to "connect" with the sheriff's dying, comatose wife.

At one point in the movie, when Powder is at the carnival with his love interest, he explains to her that the reason why people are so messed up is because they see themselves as separate from each other and separate from everything. They think in terms of "distinctions" instead of "oneness." He explains that if we could only see that underneath there is no distinction and we are all one, then we would live in harmony and love. In this viewpoint, redemption is achieved through eliminating all distinction in our thinking.

In *Phenomenon* George sees more and more clearly as he gains his freakish knowledge and tries to reach out to the community by answering their questions. He tells them that his telekinetic abilities are not voodoo, because "everything is made up of living energy. . . . It's a kind of dance." It's a dance between the energy in him and the energy in the object—"a partnership," he calls it. He then tells them that the largest living organism in the world was discovered to be a grove of aspen trees in Colorado. Investigators found out that all the trees were "one giant organism with the same root system." It would be hard to find a film that makes a stronger pitch for the supposed underlying oneness of all things.

 **Director's Cut**

Visit ‹www.godawa.com› for a critique of the monism represented in *Phenomenon* and *Powder.*

Emergent Evolution in the Movies

The Thirteenth Floor (1999) is a highly advanced filmic version of the computer game Sim City. In this movie the hero, who thought he was the first to create a virtual world with virtual characters who evolve in their independence, comes to realize that he himself is a virtual creation of someone else's computer and has only recently become self-aware.

This neoevolutionary idea of consciousness emerging out of natural processes or the inherent properties of matter is called "self-organization." It is a reduction of consciousness or spirit to physical properties.

Ironically, in *The Thirteenth Floor,* the protagonist and his love interest end up in a virtual "heaven" at the end of the movie—a happy, futuristic paradise with a sun shining perpetually on an limitless seashore. This "scientific" vision ends up being expressed in religious terms, which illustrates how difficult it is to eliminate the religious impulse inside us all.

Bicentennial Man (1999), starring Robin Williams, is another science-fiction story of emergent evolution. Adapted by Nicholas Kazan from the novel *The Positronic Man* by staunch evolutionary believer Isaac Asimov, this film is the tale of a robot's two-hundred-year journey to become a human being.

Robin Williams plays Andrew Martin, an android servant purchased by a family in the future who begins to develop emotions and creativity. By a strange anomaly (read: "evolutionary mutation"), he develops the capacity for emotions and falls in love with his owner's daughter, played by Embeth Davidtz. Through sheer accumulation of data and learning of the human condition, he develops into a sentient individual who ultimately demands his legal right to recognition as a human being. Andrew's "descent with modification," as he transplants lifelike internal organs into his body, is an obvious mirror of evolutionism.

Eventually, Andrew becomes self-aware and uses the concept of "I" to refer to himself rather than the programmed, impersonal "one." He then tries to "fulfill his destiny" by searching out companionship like a kinder, gentler version of Frankenstein. True to the materialist presupposition that intelligence is reducible to mere organized complexity, Andrew is said to be "every bit as complex" as humans (and therefore no different). By the end of the film, Andrew argues for legal acceptance as a human from the judicial powers that be. He wins and "dies" a "human being" rather than live as an immortal robot.

The last line of the film belongs to the woman Andrew "loved" as she lies dying. She says to him, "I'll see you soon," as if the robot will also live on in an afterlife. The true meaning, of course, is that even the afterlife is a concept that has been fabricated by evolved organisms as an extended desire for survival.

The question of what makes us human is broached with a more self-reflective darkness in *A.I.: Artificial Intelligence* (2001), Steven Spielberg's adaptation of Stanley Kubrick's original film concept. This homage to Kubrick is the story of a little robot boy, David (played by Haley Joel Osment), on a quest to become human. While the blatant references to Pinocchio throughout the film emphasize David's quest as a metaphor for our own dilemma of humanity, there is a quantum leap of difference between the original and the modern deconstruction of that myth.

The original *Pinocchio* was a morality tale, a purely allegorical story about good behavior and good choices being the defining characteristics of a child worthy of love. In today's climate of scientism, many actually believe that it is possible for consciousness to emerge out of mechanical complexity. In this context the Pinocchio quest is no longer a metaphor but a literal ethical question: What makes us different from any highly complex mechanical device? If we can create artificial intelligence, how is our intelligence any less "artificial"? *A.I.* attempts to answer this question with the simple maxim that to love and be loved is what makes us human.

Following in the footsteps of the lead characters in *Frankenstein* and *Blade Runner*, the robot boy David is not merely searching for the Blue Fairy to become human; he is also searching for his creator. But his creator cannot help him. The scientist who manufactured David represents the view that the abstract ability to seek after what one cannot see is what makes us human. We create myths or fairy tales in order to give meaning to our lives. Mythology here is the symbolizing of what we do not understand into larger-than-life, transcendent images. Thus David remembers that the first thing he saw upon his "birth" was an angelic figure with wings. We discover later that this apparent religious image was in fact the logo of the corporation that created him.

In this movie religion and myth are reduced to natural explanations. There is no spiritual or transcendent aspect to our existence. Even the terms for the robots ("mechas") and humans ("orgas") reflect this reduction of life forms to mechanical or organic complexity. David seeks after the Blue Fairy to make him a real boy, which we all know is not going to happen because the Blue Fairy is a Disney construct. But this abstract belief compels him onward, with religious fervor, to find the myth as truth.

By finding and deciphering the abstract literary clue left at Professor Know-It-All's vendor machine (a *Wizard of Oz* symbol), David is able to find his maker at "the end of the world, where the lions cry," which is the mythical way of describing the scientific creator's lair in the flooded remains of Manhattan city. So David's ability to find meaning in myth, to symbolize what he does not understand into mythological constructs, to seek after that which cannot be seen, is what makes David "human" to the scientist. Humanity's spiritual quest is unveiled as an arbitrary symbol-creating enterprise.

But David is not satisfied. In fact, he is in despair. So he casts himself into the sea in angst-ridden resignation. At the bottom of the ocean, he stumbles upon Coney Island, now underwater from the risen oceans, and prays to the Blue Fairy statue he finds in Pleasure Island Park to make him a real boy. The statue, by now an obvious icon of Virgin Mary, does not "answer" his prayers, and he remains in unbroken devout gaze and unsatisfied longing until his batteries run out. This is a visual reference to the filmmaker's perception of humanity's tenacious, yet ultimately vain, religious quest. And that vanity of religion is further emphasized when David finally touches the Blue Fairy, that symbol of divinity, at the end of the movie, and it crumbles into dust. Earlier, David's robotic partner, Gigolo Joe, had explained in the front of a church that sooner or later the women who go there become dissatisfied with their spiritual quest and end up in his physical arms for "real" affection and love.

Two thousand years later, when all of humankind has died out and only machines remain, some highly advanced robots, looking very much like the popular conception of alien beings, are able to "resurrect" David (recharge his batteries) and even give him his dream of "resurrecting" his original organic "mother" from her DNA for one day in order to experience her love (more religious concepts naturalized). At the end of the day, when his mother is about to go to sleep and awaken nevermore, she tells David that she loves him and has always loved him. This finally satisfies David and he is able to lie down and die with her in happiness, knowing that he is now human because he has loved and been loved. This final shot of him closing his eyes and being able to die is very important because early in the movie it was established that David did not close his eyes to sleep because he didn't have to sleep. The fact that he now closes his eyes is the evidence that he has become human and can die in peace as a human, having found his meaning.

Some may find in *A.I.* an analogy to the Judeo-Christian notion of God creating human beings as creatures whose humanity is defined in being loved by their Creator as well as others. In the first scene of *A.I.* the scientist speaking to his class of students makes this very comparison of God creating Adam to love and be loved. But with all its religious imagery and references, *A.I.* is more fittingly a humanistic interpretation of our personal quest for meaning being found in loving and being loved by other people, as well as our manufacturing of myth (including God) as a means of explaining what we do not scientifically understand. *A.I.* is a deconstruction of religious belief

 **Director's Cut**

For a book-length Christian assessment of the spiritual essence of human nature (substance dualism), see J. P. Moreland and Scott B. Rae, *Body & Soul: Human Nature & the Crisis in Ethics* (Downers Grove, Ill.: InterVarsity Press, 2000). For further reading about the nature of human identity (the mind-body problem), as well as artificial intelligence and emergent evolution, go to ‹www.godawa.com›.

into mythical construct,[3] and it revisits the evolutionary conclusion that consciousness naturally emerges out of the inherent properties of matter, that humanity can actually be achieved by a highly complex machine.

Neo-Darwinism in the Movies

The computer-animated *Dinosaur* (1999), written by John Harrison and Robert Nelson Jacobs, is a clever expression of the newer neo-Darwinian notion of evolution through cooperation rather than the old Darwinian competition.

Director's Cut

My website ‹www.godawa.com› includes a critique of the evolutionary psychology of cooperation.

After a meteor hits the earth and destroys the prehistoric Edenic environment, the dinosaurs must seek out a new "promised land" in which to live. But as they go on their journey, they are hunted down by the big, bad carnivores.

They begin their journey, squabbling with self-interest and allowing the weaker animals to be overrun and consumed by the "competitive" predators, those terrible lizards. But after a Moses-like herbivore encourages them to cooperate, they learn that they will survive through helping one another rather than competing for survival.

Dinosaur thus embodies the theory of evolutionary psychology that cooperation rather than competition is a trait of survival of the fittest.

Neopaganism in the Movies

Neopaganism is a worldview steeped in the occult sciences. Traditionally, occultism is known for its spiritual emphasis and supernatural power orientation, along with a "secret knowledge" approach to redemption. Those who are initiated into a secret knowledge of the truth are enlightened and find a personal harmony with nature and the ability to wield nature magically for their own purposes. Since Nature is a feminine deity in this view,

---

[3]Even in the final scene, in which David does meet the Blue Fairy, she is really an illusion constructed by the advanced robots to meet David's desire in his own terms rather than in terms of "reality."

New Age goddess religion is a large part of many occultic rites.

Rather than mere gender equality before the law, neopaganism seeks the overthrow of Judeo-Christianity, in which men are the leaders in the home and public roles.[4] The Wiccan religion is simply modern witchcraft and embodies the neopagan worldview. Wicca rejects the monotheistic religion of Christianity as male and therefore oppressive. Wicca is pantheistic, worshiping many little gods that are all subordinate to the ultimate goddess, sometimes referred to as "Sophia" (the Greek term for wisdom).

A New Age twist to the goddess cult is the belief that the earth itself is a living organism with a feminine spirit or consciousness. This spirit is called "Gaia" (the name of the earth goddess in Greek and Roman mythology). *Final Fantasy: The Spirits Within,* the photorealistic animated movie, is a sci-fi interpretation of this Gaia hypothesis. The Gaia spirit of the earth fights back against environmentally destructive humanity by creating deadly phantom spirits to kill humans.

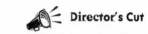 **Director's Cut**

Go to ‹**www.godawa.com**› for further examination of the New Age concept of Gaia.

The key to Wiccan or neopagan redemption is the casting off of Christianity, with all its patriarchy, rationality and control, in favor of a free-spirited, feminine chaos of nature. The Christian God is a "sky god," so Wiccans in contrast worship nature and the earth (Gaia). This is why Wiccans are often environmentalists and New Agers.

Witchcraft is ritualistic and therefore a heavily symbol-oriented sacramental system. Wiccans engage in "drawing down the moon" ceremonies (another antithesis to the Christian "sun God," as they call him), indulge

---

[4]Neopaganism shares a disdain for patriarchy with more traditional forms of feminism. Of course, what is often portrayed as patriarchy (abusive, lecherous, traitorous men) is actually *the abuse* of patriarchy rather than the true form of it. In feminist movies most men are portrayed as weaklings, scoundrels, brutes or hypocrites, and the women are usually the only ones capable of quality human relationships. See, for instance, *The Color Purple* (1985), *Thelma and Louise* (1991), *Fried Green Tomatoes* (1991), *The Piano* (1993), *G.I. Jane* (1997), *Girl, Interrupted* (1999) and *Dr. T. and the Women* (2000).

in ceremonial "Sabbat" celebrations of the changing of the seasons, and engage in rituals of "magick" to harness the power of nature for their own benefit (as opposed to "magic," which is tricks of illusion).

Wicca is popping up in mainstream movies like *The Craft* (1996), *Practical Magic* (1998), *Chocolat* (2000) and *The Cell* (2000). Anticult author Tal Brooke points out that some acceptable forms of "good" witchcraft are already adopted on television with *Charmed* and *Sabrina, the Teenage Witch*. He quotes Carol LeMasters, a witch author, about feminist origins and elements of Wicca:

> Alienated from Judaism and Christianity for their male biases, feminists of the late 1960s and early 1970s were searching for an alternative. They drew from a variety of sources, the most influential of which was Wicca. Women took from the Craft not only its worship of a goddess but its respect for nature, magical practices and ritual structure. Celebrations of moons and Sabbaths, casting circles, raising energy, chants and dances, candles and incense—all came from neopagan and Wiccan groups flourishing at the time.[5]

The Cell, written by Mark Protosevich, is a Wiccan neopagan story of occultic redemption, or in other words, liberation from the "evil," patriarchal religion of Christianity. Jennifer Lopez is Catherine, a psychoanalyst who must enter the mind of a comatose killer in order to discover the whereabouts of his last victim, still alive, hidden in a building somewhere.

When Catherine enters the killer's mind, she is accosted by bizarre, dreamlike images that represent his patriarchal upbringing. And this patriarchy is the ultimate cause for the suppression of the killer's "inner child," represented quite literally as an innocent little boy flitting around painfully confused in the dark recesses of his mind.

We see suns and moons rise and fall in time-lapse synchronicity—an expression of the cyclical birth and death veneration of nature worship. She encounters images of the killer's abusive father baptizing him cruelly

---

[5]Tal Brooke, "Spellbinding a Culture: The Emergence of Modern Witchcraft," *SCP Journal* 24, no. 4 (2000): 8.

as a child (more anti-Christian symbols), leading him to an epileptic seizure. She sees a horse dissected and sliced up into coldly rational Cartesian slices. She encounters Roman Catholic medieval tortures and the like. All of these are hideous expressions of masculine religion.

In order to defeat the killer, she lures him into her own mind and overpowers him with her goddess power, expressed in Wiccan symbols. She is all decked out as the goddess and engages in an abbreviated ceremony of drawing down the moon. With the neopagan god Pan in the background, she crucifies the killer, who is portrayed as a hunterlike "horned god," thus expressing the triumph of the free-spirited feminist goddess over the old patriarchal Christian God of violence and domination.

Read this quote from famous witch Starhawk to catch the Wiccan occultic allusions in *The Cell:*

> The horned God, the most male in the conventional sense, of the Goddess projections, is the eternal Hunter, and also the animal who is hunted. He is the beast who is sacrificed that human life may go on, as well as the sacrificer, the one who sheds blood. He is also seen as the sun, eternally hunting the moon across the sky. The waxing and waning of the sun throughout the seasons manifest the cycle of birth and death, creation and dissolution, separation and return.[6]

All this neopagan symbolism is certainly not a magical incantation that will seize the soul of the viewer by merely watching it. But it is important to recognize what symbols are being absorbed by our culture, because symbols carry powerful underlying effects on our collective culture. The acceptance of neopagan symbols in a society marks the emerging acceptance of new ideas, new philosophies, new religions.

Neopaganism can be seen as the driving force behind the Oscar-nominated *Chocolat* (2001), written by Robert Nelson Jacobs from Joanne Harris's novel. In this clever version of neopagan redemption, an entire French town is oppressed by the moral scruples of a patriarchal Roman

---

[6]Quoted in ibid., p. 12.

Catholic mayor. The town is then scandalized by the arrival of a mysteri-ous single mother, who rejects the mayor's "conventional" religion in favor of her Mayan mother's pagan origins. She arrives in the middle of Lent, no less, and opens a chocolate shop.

Chocolate is a metaphor in the film for forbidden passions, and soon the chocolate seller turns the town upside down with her free-spirited-ness. She helps a physically abused wife to leave her husband and empower herself in feminist fashion. The mayor opposes her and attempts to reform the wife beater along traditional religious lines, also known as Christian repentance.[7] His attempts fail, showing the inade-quacy of Christianity to solve the problem. But the mayor continues on in his obsessive campaign against her and the "immoral" gypsies she keeps company with, until he can no longer hold back his own passions for the chocolate she wields. He finally gives in and con-sumes the brown stuff with Dionysian abandon, learning that so-called intoler-ance and old-time Christian religion are no match for the alleged "freedom" of femi-nist neopagan liberation.

Director's Cut

Further reading examining the neopagan worldview is available at ‹www.godawa.com›.

The World in Dramatic View

If this exploration of different worldviews presented in movies proves anything, it is that the storytellers of cinema are engaging in their craft with an intent to communicate their view of the world and how we ought or ought not to live in it. They have discovered the power of a well-told story combined with a well-thought-out philosophy that is creatively embodied in the story through character, plot and image. In the same way that worldviews involve a network of individual ideas that are intercon-nected to serve a greater philosophical interpretation of our experience,

---

[7]Christians who reject occultic witchcraft as demonic are often demonized themselves in such movies as *The Scarlet Letter* (1995) and *The Crucible* (1996).

so movies are a network of events, images and themes that serve a unified way of interpreting our experience through the effective means of drama.

Watch and Learn

1. Watch *Serendipity* with some women and men together. Discuss the ways in which the fate language mirrors Christian language about God. In what ways does the fate language differ? What is the movie saying about passion and spontaneity in relationships versus commitment and loyalty? In what ways do you agree or disagree with this conclusion? How did you feel about the fiancés of the main characters and how serendipity affected them?

2. Watch *Chocolat* with men and women together. Discuss the ways in which the movie portrays moral and immoral people. In what ways is it inaccurate or stereotypical? Stereotypes usually arise from an imbalanced portrayal of exclusively negative or exclusively positive character traits. Choose one of the characters in the story (the mayor, the French woman, the young priest) or the groups of people (the gypsies, the townspeople) and discuss whether you think they are stereotypical or not. If they are stereotypical, how would you make their portrayal more realistic? What do you think is the correct biblical response to the French woman and her temptations entering the town? What do you think is the correct biblical response to the gypsies? What do you think is the correct biblical response to the wife-beating husband?

Part ③

Spirituality
in the Movies

6 Christianity

In *Hollywood Versus America* Michael Medved aptly details the film community's assault on the Judeo-Christian faith. He describes how studios willingly create negative images of religious people without a corresponding balance of positive treatments. Medved details how many movies of the 1980s created stereotypical images of Jews and Christians by casting them as buffoons, hypocrites, repressed adulterers, killers and the like.[1]

And that approach to representing Christians has not ceased since the publication of Medved's book. Movies like *Poltergeist II* (1986), *The Handmaid's Tale* (1990), *The Rapture* (1991), *Cape Fear* (1991), *Guilty as Charged* (1991), *Copycat* (1995), *Seven* (1996), *The Cell* (2000), *The Pledge* (2001) and others portray Christians as crazed, Bible-quoting kill-

---

[1]Michael Medved, *Hollywood Versus America* (New York: HarperCollins, 1992), pp. 50-90.

ers. Christianity becomes a dangerous belief that breeds and feeds murderous hearts.

A recent case in point: *Hannibal*. In this upside-down "Christ story," Mason Verger—the twisted, bitter surviving victim of Lecter—is obsessed with catching the cannibal and feeding him to flesh-eating pigs in revenge. Mason also happens to speak the evangelical language of redemption to FBI agent Clarice Starling: "You know, I thank God for what happened. It was my salvation. Have you accepted Jesus, Agent Starling? Do you have faith?" So the only person more vile, more despicable than Hannibal himself is the "Christian."

In *The Cell,* as discussed earlier, the heroine tracks down a demented killer of women whose twisted acts of evil are tied to his Christian upbringing. His method of drowning his female victims is based on his father holding him down too long when he was baptized, an act that symbolizes the forceful oppression of Christianity. The scene shows a crowd of hand-waving evangelicals "praisin' the Lord." And in true stereotypical fashion, the religious father was also criminally abusive to his family. So Christianity is at the heart of the problem of this maniacal killer.

In *Quills* (2000), playwright Doug Wright portrays the sadistic Marquis de Sade as an oppressed victim of a puritanical religious society. Of all the debauched perversions in the movie, the most heinous sexual sin, that of necrophilia (sex with a corpse), is engaged in by the Catholic priest who is trying to rehabilitate the marquis. The despicable act is only a nightmare of the priest's, but the point is still made with spite: Christians are the most vile of sinners because they "repress" their desires, which results in an oppressive society.

According to many Hollywood movies, Christianity does not merely lead to mental breakdown in serial killers; it also leads to a breakdown of society. In the secular mindset, restraining immorality unleashes the very thing it tries to stop. Repressing our desires is bad; indulging them is good. Thus saith Freud. Commitment to biblical law leads to lawlessness, like that of the legalistic, Bible-thumping warden of *The Shawshank Redemption* (1994). Reinforcing Christian moral codes in society leads to intolerance, violence, wife beating, the oppression of women and murder as in *The Scarlet Letter* (1995), *The Crucible* (1996) and *Chocolat*. Christian commitment to fidelity strangles true love as in *Jude* (1996), *The Scarlet Letter* and *The Crucible*. And trying to redeem others through missionary efforts leads to their enslavement and destruction as in *Black Robe* (1991), *At Play in the Fields of the Lord* (1991), *Jude* and *Oscar and Lucinda* (1997). Christians are portrayed in these movies as ignorant, puritanical oppressors of those they seek to convert—and as more in need of conversion themselves.

At Play in the Fields of the Lord (1991), by Hector Babenco, portrays Christianity as powerless against the glories of primitive animistic religion. It is the story of naive small-town missionaries who enter the Amazon to try to convert one of the indigenous tribes of natives untouched by civilization. The task becomes too formidable, and one missionary woman goes insane because her self-righteous faith cannot cope with the primal jungle. Her husband changes his original intentions and concludes that it would have been better for the natives if they had never met the evangelists. Another missionary accepts the temptation of lust as more desirable than her spiritual pursuit. In a complete reversal of Genesis, she confesses to another missionary that she was seduced by a certain man after bathing in the river and she felt "naked and *not* ashamed." The lead missionary is a self-righteous hypocrite who slips into a TV evangelist mode of delivery when he tries to preach the good news, all the while remaining entirely irrelevant and entirely ignorant of the people's true needs. And they all bring death, disease and destruction to the very people they are trying to save—not without blaming the Christian God for it all and likening Jesus to the devil.

Amistad (1997), David Franzoni's story of the 1839 revolt of Africans on the slave ship *Amistad* and their subsequent trial on American soil, is a revisionist denial of the major role of Christians in the abolitionist movement to free the slaves. The historically dominant force of liberation, the Quakers, are relegated to the role of kooky protesters in the background chanting irrelevant slogans and remaining blatantly unconnected to their modern world.

But despite the negative treatment that the Quakers receive, *Amistad* contains one of the most thorough descriptions of the gospel from Genesis to John that has ever been shown in a movie. A couple of the slaves get a Bible, and since they cannot read, they page through the engravings from Old to New Testament and "read" the gospel in pictures. It is a long, powerful and moving scene that transcends the political message forced upon it by the filmmakers.

Oscar and Lucinda, written by Laura Jones from Peter Carey's novel, stars Ralph Fiennes and Cate Blanchett in the title roles. This is a story about two star-crossed lovers who are addicted to gambling. The problem is that Oscar is also an Anglican minister who is tormented by his Christianity. Oscar's father is portrayed as an intolerant, legalistic, pleasure-hating Plymouth Brethren who won't let Oscar enjoy Christmas pudding because desserts are "the food of Satan." Then Oscar's Anglican adoptive father turns out to be a repressed gambler himself, who ends up committing suicide. And every denomination is intolerant of the others.

In this film Christianity is a guilt-inducing faith that haunts Oscar and Lucinda all their lives. Oscar becomes so obsessed with guilt that by the end of the film he is asking for forgiveness of sins committed by others against him! He tries to deliver a glass church, on behalf of his love for Lucinda, to a minister in the uncharted wilderness. It is floated upstream on a raft, and one day, after he has prayed inside the church (which looks like a large cage), it starts to sink into the river with him locked inside. He drowns in it as it reaches the bottom, and the point is made through metaphor that Christianity is a cage that suffocates and destroys its adherents with unnecessary guilt and intolerance.

One of the few movies critical of Christians that is worthy of some respect is *The Big Kahuna* (1999), written by Roger Rueff. It's a movie about three salesmen who come together at an industrial lubricant convention in order to wine and dine a "big kahuna" prospect into placing an order of their product that will save their floundering company.

Danny DeVito's character, Phil Cooper, has gotten to the point in his life where he is encountering the meaninglessness of his existence and his wrecked marriage. He's searching for a reason to live. Larry Mann, played by Kevin Spacey, is a spiritually void, soulless, manipulative salesman, who also happens to be a devoted friend to Phil. Out of his own spiritual vacuum he gives worthless advise to the empty, soul-searching De Vito—but he cares.

Another coworker, Bob Walker (played by Peter Facinelli), is there for his first convention. He is a young, inexperienced salesman but also a Christian who boldly shares his faith and values with others. Unfortunately, his youth betrays a judgmental spirit toward the godless. The worldly Spacey and spiritual Facinelli are soon battling for De Vito's soul and arguing over the answer to his emptiness as well as the ethical dilemma of manipulating their potential buyer into a sale. They escalate to the point of a fight and break up. The story ends with De Vito, even in his state of despair, teaching the kid a lesson that Jesus is not a product to sell to people. If you believe you have what people need, you've got to care about them if you want them to listen to what you have to say. In a sense, the young man's witnessing practices are no different than Spacey's opportunistic manipulation of the sale. We are not salesmen for Jesus; we are doctors of the soul.

Christ-Affirming Films

Although films portraying Christians in a negative light are all too common, there are some films in recent memory that deserve recognition for their honest or fair portrayal of the faithful. And it is here that recognition is needed to balance the all-too-prevalent complaining of Christian media critics. Some movies of the past, like *Chariots of Fire* (1981) and *The Mission* (1986), redeem the Christian missionary as an honorable soul with a virtuous heart who brings redemption—not destruction—to the lost. Others, like *The Apostle* (1997), show the believer as flawed but sincere. *Shadowlands* portrays Christianity as a belief of strong intellects like C. S. Lewis, and *Les Misérables* (1998) characterizes Christian forgiveness as "muscular faith" rather than weak capitulation. Some, like

Keeping the Faith (2000) and *The Apostle,* are a mixed blessing of positive and negative understandings of the faith. A survey of some of these daring films will help offset the winds of bigotry blowing hard against the gates of heaven.

Les Misérables, starring Liam Neeson as Jean Valjean, is one of the most robust stories of Christian redemption ever allowed to grace the cinema. It was adapted from the classic Victor Hugo novel by Rafael Yglesias and is through and through a parable of the nature of grace and forgiveness. Valjean is a man haunted by "the law" as embodied in Javert, played by Geoffrey Rush.

In the beginning of the story Valjean is a paroled ex-convict who restarts his life of crime by stealing a cleric's silver. When he is caught and brought back, the cleric denies it was theft and offers Valjean the silver candle stands as well. The cleric leans in and whispers to Valjean that with that silver he's ransomed him from fear and hatred, and now he must live his life for God. Because of this encounter with grace and forgiveness, reminiscent of Christ's own ransom for us, Valjean's life is forever changed. Grace is something that we do not ask for or even have the power to accept; rather, it is something that is done to us and to which we respond with repentance.

Valjean reforms and becomes a productive economic, civil and moral force in his city. But his attempt to put his past behind him is endangered by the appointment of Javert to the position of police captain in his city. Javert soon recognizes Valjean and spends the rest of the story seeking out ways to bring him down. Near the end, Valjean captures Javert but then lets him go in mercy. And in the final confrontation, when Javert has captured Valjean, he cannot kill him, because of the mercy that he had received. Javert says to Valjean, "I have tried my whole life to keep every law." Then Javert lets Valjean go, handcuffs himself and drowns himself in the river. Javert is clearly the symbol of works righteousness and the law's relentlessly condemning power (God's law, that is), along with its inability to redeem people. *Les Misérables* is a parable of what the apostle Paul meant when he said,

There is now no condemnation for those who are in Christ Jesus. For the law of the Spirit of life in Christ Jesus has set you free from the law of sin and of death. For what the Law could not do, weak as it was through the flesh, God did: sending His own Son in the likeness of sinful flesh and as an offering for sin, He condemned sin in the flesh, so that the requirement of the Law might be fulfilled in us, who do not walk according to the flesh but according to the Spirit. (Romans 8:1-4)

Sling Blade, referred to earlier as a Christ myth story, is a welcome reversal on the Christian-as-villain theme. In this story of a simpleton released from a mental hospital and trying to start his life over, Karl (a Forrest Gump-type hero) believes in God and is pro-life. He carries a Bible around and is loving and charming. The violent boyfriend of Karl's woman friend is an atheist and lives a drunken, lascivious life. In this story, belief is linked with a good life, and unbelief with a bad life.

Another movie that dramatizes Christian conversion in a muscular way is the art-house film *The Addiction* (1995), which was created by the writer/director team of Nicholas St. John and Abel Ferrara. In *The Addiction,* vampirism is used as a metaphor for humankind's growing addiction to evil along with our inability to become good. The hero of the story, Kathleen (played by Lili Taylor), a philosophy student at NYU, descends deeper and deeper into her vampirism and depravity and finds that human philosophy cannot adequately explain sin or evil but actually produces it and justifies it. A fellow vampire (Annabella Sciorra) complains with typical blame-shifting unbelief:

> **R.C. Sproul said we're not sinners because we sin; we sin because we are sinners. In more accessible terms, we're not evil because of the evil we do, but we do evil because we are evil. Yeah. Now what choices do such people have? It's not like we have any options.**

In a powerful scene characterizing the essence of sin and humankind's rebellious nature, Kathleen faces her need for repentance and goes into a raging fit against God, screaming, "I will not submit! I will not submit!"

It is not until she has gorged on the destruction of others and reaches her lowest point that she faces her need and repents, confessing faith in God for forgiveness. She is spiritually reborn into freedom, and she muses over the gravestone of her old, dead, vampiric self, "To face what we are in the end. We stand before the light, and our true nature is revealed. Self-revelation is annihilation of self."

One movie that in recent years has attempted to give a positive spin on Christian faith is *The Apostle*. Robert Duvall took more than ten years to get the movie made and has explained in interviews that he was deliberately trying to break the Elmer Gantry stereotype of Christian preachers in the South. And in fact, this interesting and faithful portrayal of the southern Pentecostal subculture is one of the few films that manage to capture the uniqueness of a Christian subculture's adherents without mocking or deriding them. Characters may be eccentric or lovable and humorous, but not laughable. The movie conveys a genuine respect for the subculture.

The story is about Eulis ("Sonny") Dewey, a preacher in Texas whose safe life is shattered when he discovers that his wife is having an affair with the local youth minister. Sonny responds by beating his wife's lover with a baseball bat, putting him in a coma. Sonny becomes a fugitive, fleeing to Louisiana, where he starts preaching under a false name and baptizes himself as an "apostle" of the gospel.[2] He struggles with God and with his conscience but continues to do the one thing he is gifted at: preaching the gospel.

Sonny helps rebuild an old church and even brings a local racist to his knees in repentance in one of the most moving Christian conversion scenes ever filmed. This film would be a strong picture of true Christian repentance, had it not been for its ending. Sonny never repents for his criminal act of violence done in the beginning. He is ultimately tracked down and caught and willingly goes to jail, *but he*

---

[2]Claiming apostleship in this postapostolic era is something the Bible doesn't allow individuals the authority to do (Acts 1:21-22), but Sonny's behavior points up the length to which self-deception will go when rationalizing our sin and pride.

never repents. True repentance would have meant he would hand himself in, thus displaying true integrity of faith and redemption. But as the movie stands, Sonny goes to jail and starts preaching the gospel there as well. No matter where he is, it comes out of him like honey from a bee. Duvall seems to be saying that the man has flaws, but at least he is sincere in his beliefs. And sincerity is the real judge of character in this fallen world.

A movie released shortly afterward, *Primary Colors* (1998), was a fictionalized retelling of Bill Clinton's pursuit of the office of president by Elaine May from Joe Klein's thinly veiled novel. The elevation of sincerity as the measure of goodness was also made in this movie of an immoral man who was a serial adulterer, pathological liar and self-seeking, Machiavellian politician. At the end of the day *Primary Colors* hammered home the point that the man, despite all his flaws, was *sincere.* He really *cared* about people. He felt their pain. And feelings, after all, not actions or conduct, are what matter in a postmodern world.

In this way, *The Apostle,* and its secular counterpart *Primary Colors,* share in a morality of the heart over a morality of behavior. The lead characters in both films engage in wicked behavior that is ultimately overlooked by the filmmakers because of these characters' sincere concern for others.

Keeping the Faith, written by Stuart Blumberg, is a unique movie that portrays both Judaism and Christianity as worthy of respect, albeit in ecumenical terms. Ben Stiller stars as a rabbi and Edward Norton as a Roman Catholic priest who both fall in love with the same woman when she comes back to town for a visit. The problem is that the rabbi can't have her because she's not Jewish and the priest can't have her because of his vows of chastity.

It's a delightful comedy that actually portrays the two religions in a cool, hip way. Their faiths are real and valuable parts of their lives. The two men walk down the streets of New York like a couple of leather-clad "God Squad" guys, known and well loved by many. They are compassionate to beggars, reach out to the minority and elderly communities,

enlarge their congregations with relevant sermons, build bridges of tolerance and acceptance between the two faiths and are just all-around funny
guys trying to "bring our religions into the twentieth century." Quite a
change from the typical Hollywood images of men of faith being
repressed, judgmental hypocrites.

The downside to *Keeping the Faith* is that their ecumenism goes
too far in their attempts to "give an Old World God a New Age spin."
The rabbi adds Hindu meditation techniques and gospel choir singing
to the temple and deconstructs the Sodom and Gomorrah episode into
a message about "God relying on us to take care of each other." This
liberal rabbi is also carelessly unaware of the Torah's prohibition
against sexual immorality, since he indulges in it with nary a second
thought or pang of conscience. But the film contains an amazing
scene of repentance when the rabbi asks for forgiveness from his congregation for dishonestly covering up his relationship with the Gentile woman.

The struggle of the priest is that he breaks down to the point of giving
up his vows to "get the girl" but fails to get her because she loves the
rabbi. But the priest rebounds when he realizes that "you cannot make a
real commitment unless you realize it is a choice you make over and over
again." This story gives a positive spin to faith as a living, breathing force
in people's lives, and for that it should be praised. But unfortunately its
ecumenical and moral compromises end up discrediting the very traditions upon which the faiths are based.
Keeping the Faith is really more about
changing faiths than maintaining fidelity
to them.

Director's Cut

**For online analyses of
"Christian" movies and
representations of Jesus in
the movies visit
‹www.godawa.com›.**

Another film that reflects positive
Christian redemption is *Fearless* (1993),
starring Jeff Bridges. Bridges's character
survives a plane crash and subsequently
gets a messiah complex, with delusions of immortality, as he "redeems"
others or helps them overcome their fears and guilt while he himself

manages to cheat death. It is not until his pride fools him into his own near-death experience that he learns he cannot save himself but must be saved by another. This movie offers a powerful metaphor for the Christian idea that we cannot save ourselves.

Paganism in the Movies

The 2000 Academy Award winner *Gladiator* marks an achievement of respectability for paganism in modern filmmaking. Writer David Franzoni has said that he deliberately wanted to offer a contrast with the sword-and-sandal epics of yesteryear:

> The film is about a hero who has morality, but that morality is a secular morality that transcends conventional religious morality. In other words, I believe there is room in our mythology for a character who is deeply moral, but who's not traditionally religious: I loved that he was a pagan, not Christian or any other traditional/established religion. All those Roman Empire movies from the '50s and '60s were religious morality plays, and had to maintain the Christian status quo, it's all very conventional. You would never have been able to portray a pagan afterlife back then, either. Maximus is a man who will die for his family, and he will die for what's right.[3]

Director's Cut

My website ‹www.godawa.com› contains further reading about atheism and secular morality.

Apparently, the contradiction of a "secular morality" derived from Roman paganism does not bother Franzoni. Maximus does "what is right" as his religion conventionally defines it for him.[4] So Franzoni has replaced the Christian convention of morality with another religious convention, that of Roman paganism, thinking that this somehow points to a secular morality that transcends

---

[3]Quoted in John Soriano, "WGA.ORG's Exclusive Interview with David Franzoni," WGA <www.wga.org/craft/interviews/franzoni2001.html>.
[4]There was nothing more conventional in Rome than the *religious* belief in Elysium and in strength and honor.

them both.[5] Be that as it may, Maximus's pagan heaven was depicted as real, which is extremely rare in a mainstream movie of such prominence, and it marks the cinematic postmodern openness to religiosity that is decidedly non-Christian.

The Spirit of Truth

As we have seen throughout this chapter, our secular society is actually a very religious one underneath. Many movies deal with spiritual themes and issues, even those of a Christian nature. Some of these Christian elements are genuine, capturing a truthful portrait of authentic Christianity. Other spiritual elements are deconstructed or reinterpreted through countervailing worldviews, but they are not ignored. The argument could be made that movies that ignore God or the spiritual side of humanity are far more dishonest than those that attack God. For when a story attacks God or tries to redefine him, it is at least admitting that he is an issue, whereas ignoring him leaves the impression that he is a nonissue, irrelevant to our reality—and those may be the most detrimental stories of all.

Watch and Learn

1. Watch *The Big Kahuna* with your church small group. Discuss what you think the theme of the movie is. Discuss how accurate or inaccurate is the depiction of the Christian in the movie. Reflect and discuss in what ways you are guilty of preaching Jesus out of salesmanship rather than

---

[5]"Transcendent secular morality" is an oxymoron. Secularity cannot be transcendent, because by definition it is immanent, that is, of the world rather than of the transcendent spiritual realm. From Aristotle to Wittgenstein, if there is one thing that the history of the secular philosophy of ethics illustrates, it is that when people reason "secularly" (from themselves), rather than from the transcendent God, they can only end in subjectivism (each person decides for himself or herself), and that is certainly not transcendent. Without a transcendent absolute standard, this secular moral relativity reduces to the will to power—whoever is in power (the majority) defines what is right and wrong for the rest (the minority). This will to power is the essence of Rome, and it is the same will to power that was embodied in the German Nazi state of the 1930s and 1940s. The director Ridley Scott understood this, and that is why he modeled the look of the Roman cult in *Gladiator* after the fascist imagery of Leni Riefenstahl's Nazi propaganda film *Triumph of the Will*.

out of genuine concern for people's souls. What kind of things can you do to continue sharing your faith without succumbing to salesmanship? Read John 4 and discuss how Jesus approached the woman at the well with the gospel. Do you think he was opportunistic? Does the Master's approach correlate in any way with a salesman's approach? How does it differ?

2. Watch *Les Misérables* with your church small group. Discuss the ways in which Valjean represents grace and Javert represents law or legalism. How is justice balanced with mercy in the Bible and in the movie?

⑦ Angels & Demons, Heaven & Hell

A hallmark of "Christian" filmmaking is its obsession with the end of the world. One would think that the book of Revelation is the most creative element of Christianity.

It all started back in 1972 with *A Thief in the Night,* which gave us scenes of the one-world government chasing after Christians in one-world government vans. But it soon grew to monstrous, bloblike proportions with *A Distant Thunder* (1978), *Image of the Beast* (1981), *The Prodigal Planet* (1983), *Revelation* (1996), *Apocalypse: Caught in the Eye of the Storm* (1998), *The Omega Code* (1999), *Revelation* (1999), *Tribulation* (2000), *Apocalypse IV: Judgement* (2001), *Megiddo: The Omega Code 2* (2001) and the granddaddy end-times moneymaking phenomenon of all time, *Left Behind: The Movie* (2001). This adaptation of the megamillion bestselling series that began as a trilogy and soon mutated into a twelve-book series has brought the book of Revelation to the forefront of popular interest.

The difficulty with this focus on end-times scenarios is the speculation that is unavoidable with such interpretations. A careful viewer who takes the time to consider these interpretations, culled from the books and media presentations of pop prophecy "experts," will soon discover that every interpretation of the Rapture, the Second Coming, Gog and Magog, the Beast with its seven heads and ten horns, Daniel's time of distress and other key prophetic elements has been changed so often due to historical events not fitting their scenarios that it is quite embarrassing.[1] Though many have surely been scared into the kingdom of God through these fantastic doomsday predictions, nevertheless, too many others have seen their unreliability and have confused the fallible interpretations of people with the infallibility of God's Word.

 **Director's Cut**

For a book-length biblical analysis of the popular end-times scenario presented in *Left Behind,* see Gary DeMar, *End Times Fiction: A Biblical Consideration of the* Left Behind *Theology* (Nashville: Thomas Nelson, 2001). My website ‹www.godawa.com› contains my perspective on "Christian" movies, a review of the film *Left Behind* and articles on end-times interpretations.

Pin the Tail on the Antichrist

Christians do not have a corner on the market of Antichrist movies. The classics *Rosemary's Baby* (1968) and *The Omen* (1976) were among the most truly scary movies about Apollyon come in the flesh. But the arrival of the new millennium seemed an acceptable time to march out new movies about the apocalypse—Hollywood-style.

The Devil's Advocate (1996), written by Jonathan Lemkin, is about a ruthless, hotshot attorney, played by Keanu Reeves, who has never lost a case and is recruited by the most powerful law firm in the world in New York. And this citadel of power just happens to be headed by Satan him-

---

[1]Dwight Wilson, *Armageddon Now: The Premillennarian Response to Russia and Israel Since 1917* (Tyler, Tex.: Institute for Christian Economics, 1991).

self, played by Al Pacino and named John Milton (an ironic jab at the seventeenth-century Christian author of the epic poem *Paradise Lost).* Of course the young lawyer doesn't know this little factoid and gets sucked in. What begins as a noteworthy Faustian bargain parable about the temptations of pride and power ultimately degenerates into an implausible tale of Satan trying to breed the Antichrist through the young hero, who it turns out is the offspring of his mother's sexual tryst with Satan.

But despite this preposterous premise, Pacino gives a rousing performance of a blame-shifting monologue worthy of the Father of Lies himself:

> **Let me give you a little inside information about God. God likes to watch. He's a prankster. Think about it. He gives man *instincts!* He gives you this extraordinary gift, and then what does he do, I swear for His own amusement, his own private, cosmic gag reel, he sets the rules in opposition. It's the goof of all time. Look but don't touch. Touch but don't taste! Taste, don't swallow. Ahaha! ... He's a sadist! He's an absentee landlord. Worship *that? Never!*

The most profound revelation of the villain is often what comes out of his own mouth, and *The Devil's Advocate* renders a truly accurate and insightful portrayal of the kinds of lies Satan may use to convince people of their innocence and rationalize their pride, avarice and vanity. At one point Milton says, "Vanity. Definitely my favorite sin. . . . Freedom, baby . . . is never having to say you're sorry."[2]

End of Days (1999), an Arnold Schwarzenegger vehicle, also features the evil one planning his big comeback, if only Arnold doesn't stop him. This movie, though predictable, has a couple of positive twists. First, there

---

[2]On the contrary, it could be argued that the favorite sin of Satan would not be vanity, as described in *Devil's Advocate,* or even disbelief in the existence of the devil, as described in *The Usual Suspects,* but the imaging of a generic, Christless God. The very essence of the Christian faith centers on the identity of Jesus Christ as God's only begotten Son, who alone is the source of salvation and author of faith (Acts 4:12). So it stands to reason that Satan's favorite sin is the belief in a God without Jesus, because *that* is a god without atonement or redemption and *that* is what populates hell in the name of heaven.

are actually priests in it who are good guys! A dark cabal of Jesuits set out to kill a woman they believe to be the one chosen to bear Satan's child, yet there is also a sect within the Roman Catholic Church that doesn't believe it is right to murder but rather that they should protect the girl.

Second, Schwarzenegger had taken the script in its earlier stages to several Christian ministers for advice, who then influenced the filmmakers to focus on the power of faith alone to defeat the devil in the end, not firearms, as was originally intended. They stressed that fleshly weapons were of no consequence to a spirit being of Satan's stature—and the filmmakers listened! The final movie has Arnold putting down his weapon and submitting to God, defeating the devil through faith, sacrificing himself to save the day.[3]

Lost Souls (2000) stars Winona Ryder as a member of a Roman Catholic team of exorcists who discover that the Antichrist is due to be revealed any day now. Of course no one believes them, especially the lonely writer who studies serial killers and, unbeknownst to him, also happens to be the "Anti-one" chosen to incarnate evil on a certain date, his 33rd birthday (just like Jesus).

One of the few good things about this Antichrist movie is that it deals with demon possession in a realistic manner. Unlike the typical *Exorcist* extravaganza of pea soup vomit and rotating heads, *Lost Souls* avoids Hollywood sensationalism by maintaining the victim's normal physical features but capturing the spiritual violence behind closed doors with a few animal sounds and minimal glimpses of the exorcists doing their duty with grave spiritual difficulty.

This naturalizing of demon possession paints a more realistic picture of the phenomenon but creates a confusing ending when the heroine must shoot said suspected Antichrist in the head, though all she has for final assurance that she's right is the number 666 flashing on the radio. This evidence is easily hallucinogenic and hardly a proof that this absolutely

---

[3]Bob Thompson, "Arnold's End-Game: Schwarzenegger Hero Seeks Redemption in End of Days," *The Toronto Sun,* November 28, 1999, p. S11.

noninfluential nobody of a writer is the ultimate unholy horror of history who is supposed to take over the world. The smallness of this identification of evil incarnate virtually deconstructs the idea into absurdity. But then again, maybe that's what they wanted to do after all.

Director's Cut

Gary DeMar offers a biblical reexamination of fulfilled prophecy and the end times in his *Last Days Madness: Obsession of the Modern Church* (Atlanta: American Vision, 1997). My website ‹www.godawa.com› provides further reading on the Beast, the Antichrist and other end-times phenomena.

Fearing Where Angels Tread

Angels have always been a great tool in movies to help bring wisdom to mortals. With the success of the hit television series *Touched by an Angel,* as well as the New Age fascination with these ethereal heavenly beings, come some recent additions to the catalog of divine celluloid assistants.

City of Angels (1998), starring Nicolas Cage and Meg Ryan, was rewritten by Dana Stevens from the original, *Wings of Desire* (1987), created by critically acclaimed born-again German filmmaker Wim Wenders. The story is about an angel who longs to experience the joys of flesh and blood, falls in love with a woman and seeks his transformation into a mortal in order to consummate those desires. It has insightful thoughts about the struggle of flesh and blood with spirit as well as some lucid images of frock-coated guardian angels doing their duties, unseen and unappreciated by their patrons.

A particularly moving scene shows an ensemble of these spiritual servants lined up on the beach watching *and hearing* the beauty of the sunrise. This is one of screendom's most beautiful visualizations of the unseen world and its inhabitants.

Seth, the angel, asks his human love interest, Maggie, to describe the taste of a pear, because he can't taste such physical things. She tries and fails to do it adequately. Then he encourages her to describe it like Hemingway, because the power of words can come so close. She finally says, "Sweet, juicy, soft on your tongue, grainy like a sugary sand that dissolves in your mouth. How's that?" He replies, "It's perfect." Watching the film reinvigorates the soul to appreciate every life experience, even the simple ones like the taste of a pear, with a thankful heart, because life is short.

The downside to *City of Angels* is its reverse Gnostic worldview. According to the Bible, the "things into which angels long to look" (1 Peter 1:12) are not the experiences of being physical but the eternal gospel of salvation, which had been prophesied but hidden for centuries. From its earliest origins, Gnosticism was a syncretistic belief system that attempted to blend elements of Platonic Greek thought and other heathen ideas with Christianity. One of its major tenets was the dualistic notion of the eternal opposition of the flesh and spirit within everyone. These two aspects of our existence are so diametrically opposed in the Gnostic worldview that they create the longing for release of the entrapped ghost from the physical body. To the Gnostic, spirit is eternally good and matter is intrinsically evil. This led one branch of Gnosticism to conclude that antinomian indulgence in the fleshly (sinful) side of life would further liberate the spirit from its physical bondage.[4]

City of Angels embraces this spirit-flesh dichotomy but adds a switcheroo by making the spirit lust for enfleshment and sensual delight rather than the flesh hungering for spiritual deliverance. And the act of sexual intercourse becomes the highest experience in this humanistic parable of the priority of this life over the next.[5] Seth says of his desire for physical connection with Maggie, "I would rather have had one breath of her hair, one kiss from her mouth, one touch of her hand, than eternity without it." Thus the highest love in life is the love of another human rather than the love of one's Creator.

---

[4]Philip Schaff, *History of the Christian Church* (Albany, Ore.: Ages Software, 1997), 2:350-57.
[5]Sex becomes the closest thing to a transcendent experience that humanists can approximate. Sex becomes a secular sacrament. This use of Christian spiritual images as humanistic metaphors to exalt humanity and this life over God and the next world is a common postmodern revision of cultural symbols. Unlike Platonism and humanism, true biblical spirituality is holistic, embracing the physical world as a worthy creation, and recognizes spiritual tension, not as separation of matter and spirit but as sinful nature and conscience convicted by the Law of God (Galatians 5:16-25).

The humanistic overturning of spirituality in favor of sensuality is not solely directed at Christian spirituality but at other religions as well. In the Eastern *Crouching Tiger, Hidden Dragon* (2000), Hui-Ling Wang, Kuo Jung Tsai and James Shamus tell the tale of master Li Mu Bai, who has struggled with his search for enlightenment through the negation of the physical world and the exaltation of the spiritual. He cannot find it because he is haunted by his long-time unrevealed love for his friend, Yu Shu Lien. The power of the flesh draws him like a deity to his course.

At the end of the movie, when Li Mu Bai is dying in the arms of his beloved, he finally says of his search for spiritual enlightenment, "I have wasted my entire life. But I have found enlightenment when at last I realize that I love you." So human love rather than spiritual love is true enlightenment.

Michael (1996), writer-director Nora Ephron's excursion into angelology, is another example of the exaltation of romance as religion. John Travolta plays the archangel with a twist. Rather than a blindingly bright, glorious creature, he is a fat, slobbish, cigarette-smoking, beer-guzzling, womanizing sugar addict, more akin to the cavorting fallen angels of the nonbiblical book of Enoch than to the glorious warrior of light and terror that he really is in the book of Daniel.

This humorous deconstruction of the biblical angel image gives Michael one last duty before expiration: returning a heart of love to a cynical sensationalist journalist, played by William Hurt. Hurt's character makes a living off of deceiving people in a *National Enquirer*-type newspaper, and he must ultimately face his own revelation of deception from the woman with whom he falls in love.

Much like Seth in *City of Angels,* Michael devours the simplest pleasures of life, like a good piece of pie, the largest ball of twine in the world and the company of women. He appreciates it all in the manner that we often fail to because we are too absorbed in our own troubles. He is determined not to allow life to be what happens when he's busy making other plans.

The Preacher's Wife (1999), written by Nat Mauldin and Allan Scott, represents a return to a more biblical image of angels as messengers sent to help humans learn the value of character and faith, similar to *It's a Wonderful Life* and *The Bishop's Wife,* the original movie upon which it is based. Denzel Washington plays an angel whose job is to turn the heart of an overworked, spiritually fatigued minister back to his wife and to the heart of his church.

Dark Angel

Another aspect of the spiritual realm that has garnered the attention of Hollywood in recent years is the notion of spiritual warfare. Made popular by the mega-bestselling Christian novel by Frank Peretti, *This Present Darkness,* not to mention the spiritual warfare movement with its "spiritual mapping" of regionalized demonic powers, this idea is definitely cinema-friendly, with angels fighting over souls and the violence that occurs with the intersection of the two worlds.

The low-budget *Raging Angels* (1995), written by Kevin Rock, David Markov and Chris Bittler, resulted in an uninspiring story of these battling spirits. The inadequacy of this movie is evidenced by the fact that the director is named Alan Smithee, a pseudonym used by directors when they lose control of a film and consider it damaging to their reputation.

A more successful portrayal of angelic armed conflict is the low-budget *The Prophecy* (1995), which spawned two sequels as a result of its success. In this story Christopher Walken, playing the archangel Gabriel, is planning another "fall from heaven," like his predecessor Lucifer, because of his anger at God's "unjust" control of the universe. The problem is that the angels' rebellion allows them to snatch souls from people to keep them from entering into heaven, so God has to send in his man to stop it all. That man is a priest who has lost his faith and has become a cop (played by Elias Koteas).

Though much of the theology is not biblical, it renders some Bible-friendly images of angels (similar in vein to the long-coated, sword-toting immortals of *Highlander).* It also forthrightly deals with the uncomfortable scriptural fact, frequently ignored by the pious, that angels have often been sent by God to bring death to multitudes of people.

The hero, in a state of unbelief, explains why he turned from God. But even in his unbelief he unwittingly recounts a biblical truth, namely that God's prerogative is to do as he pleases, without being obligated to explain anything to anyone (see Job 40—41; Romans 9:14-24). The priest-turned-cop has this to say:

 **Did you ever notice how in the Bible, whenever God needed to punish someone, or make an example, or whenever God needed a killing, he sent an angel? Did you ever wonder what a creature like that must be like? A whole existence spent praising your God, but always with one wing dipped in blood. Would you ever really want to see an angel?**

This is a sobering truth that those who consider themselves "spiritual warriors" should reconsider in their headlong pursuit of all things angelic. Angels in the Bible are awesome creatures of power that often terrify human beings, making them fall to the ground on their faces in fear (see Genesis 17:3, 17; Joshua 5:14; Daniel 8:17; 10:7).

Bedazzled (2001), a modern Faustian parable by Larry Gelbart, Harold Ramis and Peter Tolan, stars model/actress Elizabeth Hurley as a female incarnation of the Dark Lord of Sheol. She tempts innocent Elliot (played by Brendan Fraser) with seven wishes in exchange for his soul. As each wish for wealth, fame, sensitivity and intellect is ruined by unexpected complications, Elliot learns that in order to be a self-actualized person, and in order to get the girl of his dreams, he needs to engage in "selfless acts of redemption" rather than selfish pursuits of power.

This parable lucidly points out the seductiveness of temptation (Satan disguising himself quite appropriately as a female angel of beauty) and the emptiness of vanity and power with all its accouterments (à la Ecclesiastes). Unfortunately, it also ends up secularizing God into Zenlike terms as "that universal spirit that animates and binds all things in existence."

After Elliot overcomes the Hurley she-devil and they become chums (the devil knows when she's lost fair and square), she lets him in on a "little secret":

> **The whole good and evil thing. You know, Him [God] and me.**
> **It really comes down to you. You don't have to look very hard**
> **for heaven and hell. They're right here on earth. You make the**
> **choice.**

And thus the spiritual reality of temptation and eternal punishment or bliss is replaced with a humanistic substitute of heaven and hell right here and now.

Heaven and Hell

And speaking of here-and-now substitutes for heaven and hell, there are plenty more of them to be found in movies. Eternal punishment for sins is one of the most unacceptable doctrines to the unbeliever. So a common way that unbelievers deal with heaven and hell is to turn them into symbols for earthly experience.

An example of this translation of hell to earth is *Jacob's Ladder* (1990). In *Jacob's Ladder* (an obvious biblical reference), by Bruce Joel Rubin, a returning Vietnam vet is plagued by demons that turn out to be metaphors for his own personal problems

Director's Cut

For further reading on spiritual warfare, go to 'www.godawa.com'.

in need of resolution before he dies. This is a literalization of the pop psychology metaphor of "personal demons" that haunt us.

Rare is the movie that paints an accurate portrait of heaven and hell. Such comedies as *Bill and Ted's Bogus Journey* (1991), Woody Allen's *Deconstructing Harry* (1997), *South Park: Bigger, Longer and Uncut* (1999), *Little Nicky* (2000) and others mock heaven and hell or playfully use them for irreverent comedic purposes. And many horror movies, such as *Hellraiser* (1986), use hell as a mere tool for exploitation of gore, violence and evil rather than as true moral warning. But there are a few mainstream movies that have attempted to face the eternal retribution spoken of in the Bible.

Ghost (1990), by Bruce Joel Rubin, was one of the few movies in past years that depicted people actually being drawn down into hell for punishment. This in itself was a triumph in our relativistic culture that has championed the goodness of humankind and the rejection of moral judgment. Unfortunately, the New Age essence of the film was that only "bad" criminals and murderers get hell, but "good" people like the hero in love get heaven. So the biblical truth that there is no one who is good enough to go to heaven on his or her own merits (Romans 3:12) is replaced by a works salvation of the goodness within a person.

Typically, hell is interpreted as a burning fire over which Satan reigns. Movies like *Spawn* (1997) and *Bedazzled* picture God and the devil more in Zoroastrian terms of two nearly equal powers fighting it out, Yin and Yang-like, with the results in question. Satan is envisioned as the overlord of hell who will punish people in the flames with his great power. What is missed in all this battling of spiritual forces is the biblical revelation that Satan does not rule over hell and that he does not punish people in hell; God is in charge and he does the punishing. In fact, God is going to punish Satan in hell as well (Revelation 20:10, 15).

Karma and Reincarnation

Another way of redefining heaven and hell has been the use of karma and reincarnation. The idea of karma is a substitute for true heaven and hell that is more acceptable to the modern mentality that wants to deal with responsibility for actions but doesn't want to face true punishment for sinners in the hands of an angry God (see Revelation 14:10-11). Karma is the Eastern belief, culled from Hinduism and Buddhism, that we pay for our sins, or the wrong we've done, in an impersonal, cyclical, "what goes around, comes around" kind of way. The payment exacted upon the soul is reincarnation as a lower life form than the previous life in the attempt to "get it right" the next time. We carry the burden of our past into the future.

The purpose of reincarnation is to work off the penalty for our sins in a purgatory-like fashion. It is similar to the biblical notion of reaping what we sow from our sins (Galatians 6:7), but with the added unbiblical qualification that we can work our way to heaven as we become better, more moral people through successive incarnations. Thus we each become our own savior, able to ultimately triumph over sin through our own goodness. We save ourselves. Some movies that have dealt with this reincarnation theme are *Flatliners* (1990), *Defending Your Life* (1991), *Dead Again* (1991), *What Dreams May Come* (1998) and *Down to Earth* (2001).

Dead Again, written by Scott Frank, seems to be a movie that, rather than actually promoting reincarnation as a religious doctrine, uses it as a creative storytelling tool for a thrilling plot twist. Nevertheless, reincarnation is presented as a means of redemption. By discovering what problems the characters have in past lives (like the murder that occurred in the movie), they can resolve their present problems and find peace of mind and true love.

In Albert Brooks's comedy *Defending Your Life* (1991) the hero dies and goes to Judgment City, where he must go through a trial (but "it's not really a trial," they say, avoiding the impression of crime) in order to see whether he is mature enough in spirit to go to heaven or whether he is destined to go back to earth to try again and get it right. In this story fear is the big factor in determining one's spiritual redemption. Brooks uses a "This was your life" concept of showing movies of the person's past behaviors as evidence for his "guilt" or "innocence."

As we see these movies of the hero's life, we find that his fate is based on his living too fearful of a life—too fearful to have defended himself against a bully as a child, too fearful to have invested money as a young man and too fearful to have fought for a better salary for himself as an adult, among others. These self-oriented points of judgment reduce the story to a parable of redemption through selfishness. If the hero was only more aggressive to get what he wanted in life, he would go to heaven.

What Dreams May Come (1998), written by Ron Bass from Richard Matheson's novel, is an epic adventure through heaven and hell. The hero dies and goes to heaven. But his wife, his soul mate, is in such psychic pain from her loss (in addition to losing her two children in death as well), that she commits suicide. In this movie's worldview suicides go to a hell of their own making, "not because they were immoral or selfish," but because they violate the natural order of their process of spiritual growth. They create their own hell because they are too obsessed to connect with others.

The hero, played by Robin Williams, decides to go on a quest through hell to try to bring his beloved back. As he does, we are treated to a visual feast of torments worthy of Dante himself, similar to scenes out of C. S. Lewis's *The Great Divorce*. The hero finds redemption in self-sacrifice, choosing to stay in hell with his beloved rather than going to heaven without her. This knocks her out of her self-created head trip and the two end up in heaven again, only to be reincarnated for another go at falling in love on earth.

The movie is filled with Eastern metaphysical musings about mind being the nature of reality and about physicality being only illusion. The heavens and hells people live in are creations of their own minds in a karmic universe. God is given one mention that reduces him to irrelevance. When asked by the newly dead hero where God is in all of this, the wise mentor (played by Cuba Gooding Jr.) tells him, "Oh, he's up there, somewhere, shouting down that he loves us, wondering why we can't hear him. Ya think?" Not only is God unseen and unheard, but that little "Ya think?" tacked on at the end announces God as a being without any substantial reality outside of one's subjective beliefs. An unseen, unheard, unknown God is really the same as no God at all.

An interesting alternative ending on the DVD reveals with more clarity the intentions of the authors. The mother who committed suicide is about to go back to earth in order to work through her bad karma from suicide because, the hero is told, "There is a reason every religion in the world talks about atonement. Because we know inside we need to take responsibility for what we've done." The responsibility and atonement portrayed in *What Dreams May Come* are reduced to more of a therapy than a punishment.

Flatliners (1990), written by Peter Filardi, uses karma as a concept more akin to the Christian notion of sin and repentance than do the other movies. The story is about several med students who secretly explore near-death experiences by stopping their hearts and reviving them. As the students come closer to death, their real lives become haunted by sins they've done in the past—sexual promiscuity, racism, hatred and bullying. As these waking nightmares become life threatening, one of the characters decides to address his fault of racism and hatred by making amends with the black woman he harmed when they were in grade school. This repentance dissolves the surreal attacks. Their sins have come back to haunt them (reaping what they've sown), and their redemption lies in repentance.

While faith in God is regrettably avoided in this redemption, it is still a good example of one half of the equation of true redemption (see Acts 20:21; 26:20). Rather than portraying personal weaknesses *(Defending Your Life)* or poor self-esteem *(What Dreams May Come)* as humanity's problem, *Flatliners* addresses actual sins of the characters as the issue.

 **Director's Cut**

See ‹www.godawa.com› for further examination of reincarnation.

Movies can be a powerful means of communicating spiritual realities, good or bad, true or false, as our survey has illustrated. Whether Antichrists, angels, demons or heaven and hell, the spiritual curiosity in human beings cannot be ignored and finds its way to the big screen in plenty of mainstream movies. While many of these presentations are far from biblical, they can often become inspiration for a further study of Scripture to find out the truth of the matter.

Watch and Learn

Watch one of the movies in this chapter with some friends. Discuss the interpretations of spirituality that you agree with and the interpretations you disagree with. How does the redemption portrayed coincide with biblical truth? Where does it depart from biblical truth?

 Faith

The existential leap of blind faith has already been discussed in chapter three. But this leap is not merely confined to the rejection of reason. It bleeds into the realm of the sciences as well, ultimately reducing faith to a belief in something that we think is factually untrue. As indicated earlier, this kind of faith is belief in spite of or against the evidence. In order to understand just how influential on movies this definition of faith is, we need to know where it came from and how it came to us. Then we can see how specific movies illustrate this "faith" in its various aspects.

A Necessarily Oversimplified Brief History of the Senses

In the year 1620, during the Renaissance in Europe, English jack-of-all-trades Francis Bacon published the *Novum Organum,* in which he proposed the inductive method as the basis for scientific knowledge. This procedure of inferring general laws of nature (regularity) from empirical observation and repeatable experimentation would soon prime the explosion of what we know as modern science.[1]

With the coming of Sir Isaac Newton and the British empiricists, humanity's faith in empirical observation would soon eclipse all other belief systems. Of course many still believed in God as the Creator of that observable order. In fact, as historian of science Alfred North Whitehead has stated, it was the Christian worldview that provided the philosophical foundation for the birth of science.[2] Because God is rational, his creation reflects that same rationality and lawlike regularity. We can trust that the future will be like the past ("natural laws") because God himself sustains the regularity of nature by his omnipotent power.

In the 1700s the skeptical empiricism of Scottish philosopher David Hume established doubt about the knowability of reason and morals, and even the justification of causality itself, relegating them to the realm of unjustifiable beliefs.[3] The German thinker Immanuel Kant attempted to solve this skeptical dilemma by proposing that our mind uses reason and value as tools to organize our experiences. We actually have no way of

---

[1]Bacon proposed that making logical inferences from what we observe in the world is more reliable than formulating ideas about the world apart from investigating it. If we want to know, for example, whether light is important for the growth of green plants, then we can test it. We can put some plants in darkness and others in light and then we can see what happens. This process of observation, hypothesis, experimentation and conclusion is what became known as the scientific method. Thanks to Stephen Ross for this clarification.

[2]And not merely the Christian worldview in principle, but the *medieval* Christian worldview in historical practice. The medieval period was the very era that Enlightenment thinkers consider to be the "Dark Ages." See Stanley L. Jaki, *Chance or Reality and Other Essays* (Lanham, Md.: University Press of America, 1986), p.152.

[3]The online *Oxford Companion to Philosophy* explains:

> Most philosophers hold that there is a problem about induction: its classic statement is found in Hume's *Enquiry Concerning Human Understanding*. Having observed that all arguments to unobserved matters of fact depend upon the relation of cause and effect, Hume remarks that our knowledge of this relation depends on experience: but, he goes on to argue: all inferences from experience suppose, as their foundation, that the future will resemble the past. . . . If there be any suspicion that the course of nature may change, and that the past may be no rule for the future, all experience becomes useless, and can give rise to no inference or conclusion. It is impossible, therefore, that any arguments from experience can prove this resemblance of the past to the future; since all these arguments are founded on the supposition of that resemblance. (iv. ii. 32) See <http://xrefer.com/entry.jsp?xrefid=552412&secid=.->.

knowing whether the categories of the mind actually correspond to ultimate reality, but it is convenient for us to believe so.

The bifurcation of our experiences and our minds would soon evolve into a dichotomy of "fact" and "value," facts being those things that we can empirically verify with our senses and values being those things the mind attributes abstractly to its experiences. In this view gravity is a fact, implying objective reality, while morality is a value, implying subjective relativity. We can prove facts, but we can't prove values. This dichotomy of fact and value would soon turn into a battle for social dominance in which so-called "fact" would eventually come out on top and keep pushing values to the point of irrelevancy, where they are now regarded as mere myth or cultural interpretations.

In the nineteenth century Auguste Comte had completely rejected metaphysics and theology ("values") as an adequate "means of knowledge." He developed what he called "positivism," a philosophy based on empirical knowledge and experience. By the mid-1930s, the logical positivist school had become a dominant force in society. Led by thinkers such as A. J. Ayer, Morris Schlick and Rudolph Carnap, this school relegated all metaphysical notions (including religion and morals) to the scrap heap of meaninglessness.

There was a place for believing in such things as God, doctrines and ethics, but they were not verifiable through empirical observation, the scientific method or sense perception and were therefore quite literally "nonsense" to these men. In fact, this supreme faith in our sense perception would balloon to such proportions that it is currently assumed as true that facts are "provable" things and values (morals, religion, truth) are matters of "faith" without support.

Fact and faith are often perceived as eternal opposites in our culture. People tend to think that what they can experience with their five senses is the most reliable knowledge and that religion is arbitrary, nonprovable belief. If a scientist says something, there is instant credibility; if a religious leader says something, well, that's true for him but not necessarily true for me.

So . . . when the Son of Man comes, will he find faith in the movies? Religious faith plays an important role in many modern secular movies. Because of this influence of empiricism on the Western mind, faith is usually dealt with in one of three different ways: faith versus proof, the individual versus the institution, and doubt versus faith.

Blind Faith Versus Proof

Indiana Jones and the Last Crusade (1989), written by A-list scribe Jeffrey Boam, is a movie about faith. It brings an occult angle to Christianity as a religion of mystically powered relics but weaves it together with the notion of faith as trust (very often, blind). As Indiana's lightheaded sidekick says, "The search for the cup of Christ is the search for the divine in all of us." That's occultism. And faith is ultimately a part of the nonfactual realm. As Indiana tells his class, "Archaeology is the search for fact—not truth."

At the end of the story, when Indiana is following his map to the Holy Grail, he finds himself at the edge of a great precipice. The only way to cross the chasm to the other side is to follow the drawing of a knight stepping out into midair. Indiana decides to follow this drawing by stepping into the chasm with faith, only to find there an invisible bridge that allows him to cross. Faith is here affirmed as a blind leap, or at least a blind step.

The positive side of this tale is that Indiana begins as a skeptic telling his class, "We cannot afford to take mythology at face value," but ends up a true believer in the factual origins of such myths. And Indiana's father, played by Sean Connery, says at the end that "finding the Grail is not about finding a prize, but about illumination."

Keeping the Faith (referred to earlier) has the priest giving a self-help-style sermon to his congregation with this definition of faith:

> **It's important to understand the difference between religion and faith. Because faith is not about having all the right answers. Faith is a feeling. Faith is a hunch. It's a hunch that there is something bigger connecting it all, connecting us all together. And that feeling, that hunch is God.**

So according to this movie, faith is a feeling, and that feeling is God.

Unstrung Heroes (1995), a film adapted by writer Richard LaGravenese, is the story of Steven, a boy with a scientific atheist father (played by John Turturro) who thinks "nothing is broken that science can't fix" and "science is earth's salvation." But this man of godless reason must learn that science can't fix the death of his beloved wife, and so he is left without redemption.

Meanwhile, Steven gets to know his two crazy (quite literally) and paranoid religious uncles, Danny and Arthur. Their cute and cuddly insanity becomes a metaphor for the irrationality of religion that cannot be explained by reason yet leads the child to individual freedom—a freedom that seems to violate the orderly science of his father.

At one point the dying mother scolds the atheist father by telling him, "Maybe there is a God, or maybe some of us want to believe there is." Sincerity of belief, not actual reality, is important. It's a case of emotional commitment over rationality, the heart over the head, as explained in chapter three.[4]

Another example of linking insanity with religious belief and passion is *The Messenger: The Joan of Arc Story* (1999), written by Luc Besson and Andrew Birkin. This deconstructed view of St. Joan shows an impetuous girl turn into a virtual lunatic leading a nation in the name of her bizarre religious hallucinations.

Containing an eerily brilliant performance by Dustin Hoffman as God (although he too is ultimately a self-generated illusion of Joan's subconscious), this movie is a thought-provoking depiction of the danger of those who claim that God speaks to them with a special insider relationship. And it creates an impressive ambiguity of our perception. The

---

[4]Unfortunately, the problem with making sincerity the standard of value is that it can't differentiate between right and wrong values. The sincerity of Hitler is equivalent in value to the sincerity of Mother Teresa, even though their worldviews are opposite. As soon as one makes a distinction that some kinds of sincerity are wrong and others are right, sincerity is no longer the standard. The reference point of what is right or wrong is actually the judge *over* sincerity. Value simply cannot be determined by sincerity because sincerity is a measure of commitment to a value, not the value itself.

visions seemed so real—but were they? Or are we self-deluded by our religious bias or passionate commitment to a cause?

Witness, in contrast, *Henry V* (1989), a William Shakespeare adaptation by Kenneth Branagh. In this movie the king is a man of justice and fairness who is also a man of God with true compassion for his people, his soldiers and even his enemies. The miraculous English victory on the field of Agincourt is openly acknowledged as an act of God against the proud and defiant French. Faith makes a king proceed with caution and humble reliance on God rather than the blind spiritual fervor (or is it raging insanity?) of an immature child in *The Messenger.*

An interesting flip-flop of science as a leap of faith occurs in the movie *O Brother, Where Art Thou?* (2000), by the eccentric brothers Coen (Ethan and Joel). In this amusing tale based very loosely on Homer's *The Odyssey,* but told using Christian symbols and spirituality, the accusation of blind and even ignorant faith is leveled at the empiricist, the one who denies that there is a supernatural world that transcends our physical senses.

O Brother is the story of three escaped convicts from a Mississippi chain gang in the Depression-era South led by Ulysses Everett Gill (played by George Clooney). While on the lam, they encounter an old-fashioned, fundamentalist baptism at a river. But unlike in most movies, these Bible belt people are mocked only through the eyes of the skeptical Everett, not the others. Angelic singing permeates the area with peace, and two of the convicts decide to repent and get cleansed from their past life of sins. But Everett, good ole empirical scientist that he is, believes there is a natural explanation for every religious "superstition." He refuses to join in the conversion and chalks it up to the belief that tough times brings out the weakness in people.

Everett's empiricism is ultimately shown to be blind faith itself because he keeps explaining away all the fortuitous events that happen to the three fellows. Everett's lack of spiritual understanding and his belief in the inherent goodness of humanity also keep him from recognizing real evil when faced with it. A big, one-eyed pseudo-Bible salesman (Cyclops) hoodwinks two of the convicts and robs them. The Christian convict tries to fight the ogre right in front of Everett because he has discerned his evil intentions, but the blissfully unaware Everett never catches on!

Earlier in the story, the three men hear a black man prophesy that among "many startlements" they will encounter are a flood and a vision of a cow on top of a cotton house. Everett is not in awe of such "mystery."

 The blind are reputed to possess sensitivities compensatin' for their lack of sight, even to the point of developing paranormal psychic power. Now, clearly seein' the future would fall neatly into that ka-taggery. It's not so surprisn' then.

Everett keeps on a-scoffin' at this and other spiritual things until he is on his knees at the climax of the film, about to be shot by the bad guy, and belts out a sinner's prayer to God quicker than you can shake a stick.

But when a flood sweeps through the valley and saves the convicts from their execution, they float to the top and the men yell out that God has pitied them in response to their prayers. Everett remarks with contempt that his hayseed brethren are just showing their "want for innalect." "There's a perfectly scientific explanation for what just happened," he opines. But when challenged that he has suddenly changed his tune he was just a-singin' back at the gallows, he promptly derides, "Well, any human being will cast about in a moment of stress." His foxhole conversion proves counterfeit. Just then they see a cow on a cotton house roof, as the oracle prophesied, and Everett looks the other way in denial, remaining truly blind in his empirical faith in "scientific facts."[5]

---

[5]Even if we accept the validity of science, what the average Everett doesn't comprehend is that there are as many versions of "science" as there are Christian denominations. Even what scientists have considered to be reliable knowledge has often turned out to be in error. Some have even noted that "science," as a monolithic unity of knowledge, simply does not exist. And in fact, different sciences are driven and changed by philosophical commitments and prejudices just as regularly as any other metaphysical system or religion (Thomas Kuhn, *The Structure of Scientific Revolutions* [Chicago: University of Chicago Press, 1996]). The famous quantum physicist Max Planck voiced the dirty little secret that most modern scientists refuse to admit: "Over the entrance to the gates of the temple of science are written the words: 'Ye must have faith' " (Max Planck, *Where Is Science Going?* [Woodbridge, Conn.: Ox Bow, 1981], p. 214).

The issue of blind faith in science is also explored in the movie *Contact* (1997), adapted by James V. Hart and Michael Goldenberg from the famous Carl Sagan novel of contact with extraterrestrial life through radio waves. In this movie the similarity of religious faith and scientific faith is explored through the contrast of characters Palmer Ross (played by Matthew McConaughey), a political lobbyist and "man of the cloth without the cloth [and the morals]," and Dr. Eleanor ("Ellie") Ann Arroway (played by Jodie Foster), an atheist research scientist who establishes contact with extraterrestrials.

In a spirited discussion Ellie questions the validity of faith in things one cannot see. She challenges Palmer to prove the existence of God. Unpredictably, Palmer turns Ellie's own argument against her and challenges her, "Do you love your father?" "Yes, very much," she replies. "Prove it," demands Palmer, and for one rare moment in film history, the scientist is the one without a response.

 **Director's Cut**

For a fragment on "Faith and Proof," related to this chapter, and for further reading on faith and apologetics in the context of modern thinking, visit ‹www.godawa.com›. Two valuable introductory books on Christ-focused reasoning, worldview apologetics, and the interaction of faith and reason come from Greg Bahnsen, *Always Ready: Directions for Defending the Faith*, ed. Robert R. Booth (Texarkana, Ark.: Covenant Media Foundation and American Vision, 1996); and Gary DeMar, *Thinking Straight in a Crooked World: A Christian Defense Manual* (Powder Springs, Ga.: American Vision, 2001).

True to Sagan's devoted faith in science, *Contact* explores the actual religious foundations of modern science's quest for ultimate answers. No longer are scientists content in dealing with physical phenomenon, but they are now engaged in the metaphysical quest for truth and the ontological cure for loneliness. Ellie thinks that finding extraterrestrial life somehow supplies this answer.

> For as long as I can remember, I've been searching for something, some reason why we're here. What are we doing here? Who are we? If this is a chance to find out even just a little part of that answer . . .

After Ellie makes contact with an alien in the guise of her dead father, the alien tells her the "wisdom of the ages."

> You're an interesting species, an interesting mix. You're capable of such beautiful dreams and such horrible nightmares. You feel so lost, so cut off, so alone, only you're not. See, in all our searching, the only thing we've found that makes the emptiness bearable is each other.

The Search for Extraterrestrial Intelligence (SETI) reduces to the search of lonely sentient beings for other lonely sentient beings with which to be lonely together. In an ironic twist *Contact* deconstructs SETI's search for alien life forms into a faith commitment itself. When young Ellie asks her dad if he thinks there are people on other planets, he responds, "I don't know, Sparks. But I guess I'd say if it is just us . . . seems like an awful waste of space."

And Ellie's experience with aliens is also likened to a faith encounter. She stands before a congressional committee to try to explain her wormhole space travel and she winds up looking like any other religious person trying to explain her "testimony" or religious faith encounter. What is normally criticized by atheist scientists as the arbitrariness of faith is now employed by the atheist science poster girl herself.

> Look, all I'm asking is for you to just have the tiniest bit of vision. You know, to just sit back for one minute and look at the big picture. To take a chance on something that just might end up being the most profoundly impactful moment for humanity, for the history . . . of history.

In other words, she's asking them to have *faith,* to *believe* that her experience was real and keep searching for that for which there is no evidence (except an awful lot of wasted space) in order to make the emptiness more bearable.

The Individual Versus the Institution

The image of pioneers braving the cold, cruel frontiers all alone is an American myth (discussed earlier) that has entrenched itself in every aspect of our culture. And that mythology is all about individualism.

Much good has come from such thinking, but so has much that is questionable. We Americans think we can do everything on our own from starting our own businesses to starting our own religions, and we distrust institutions as big, bad corporate entities headed by power-mongering "suits" who want to use the institution to tromp on the little guy. We love the underdog, the one person against the system, which is collectively referred to as "the man." But we also elevate "individual rights" to the exclusion of personal responsibility and in the name of freedom push those rights upon others through massive litigation. We end up with a tribalist society of warring factions—and all of it under the guise of respect for individual rights.

Individualism has also resulted in relativism and a breakdown of tradition—not just bad tradition but all tradition. Americans question *all* authority, because after all, "no one is the boss of me." This rejection of authority and institutions, or the many in favor of the few, has become a staple of religion as well. Transfers of church membership are more often attributable to personality differences than justifiable biblical separation.[6] The elevation of the individual to a nearly absolute status has affected American Christianity to the detriment of true biblical community and accountability. Everyone tends to do what is right in his or her own eyes.

Rebellion against authority plays well in American movies. Stories with a lone hero who stands against the system or doesn't fit in are more conducive to storytelling than are ensemble pieces, and they can ring true

---

[6]Rather than follow the apostle Peter's command to "submit yourselves for the Lord's sake to every human institution" (1 Peter 2:13), and especially to one's church elders (5:5), most Christians will usually just up and leave their church to find a new one that "ministers to them."

when the individual is right and the collective is wrong. But rare will be the occurrence of a hero who realizes that he is a rebel and is wrong in his individualism. It just doesn't fit our mythology of individualism. This is why most institutions of faith are portrayed in a negative way. They are usually filled with power mongers set on control and destruction, as in *The Handmaid's Tale* (1990), *The Scarlet Letter, The Crucible, Chocolat* and *Quills,* or they are boring, stuffy keepers of dead traditions, as in *Sister Act* (1992), *Oscar and Lucinda* and *Keeping the Faith.*

Two examples of this emphasis on the individual over the institution are *Stigmata* (1999) and *Simon Birch* (1998).

The main point of *Stigmata* is to show that the Roman Catholic Church has suppressed secret "gospels" of Christ that contain unconventional theology. It's a horror genre story about a young New York hairdresser, played by Patricia Arquette, who begins receiving the wounds of Christ on her body until it leads her to a secret "gospel" document hidden away by a South American priest. The Roman Catholic Church is shown as a nefarious conglomerate of religious leaders trying to suppress this document because it will blow open the credibility of the entire New Testament.

One of the phrases in the scandalous document of *Stigmata* says:

 The kingdom of God is within you and all around you. It is not within buildings of wood or stone. Split a piece of wood and you will find me. Look beneath a stone and I am there.

The real-life source material of this fictional text is the Gospel of Thomas from the Nag Hammadi library, a collection of Gnostic literature written sometime after the first century. While it is true that God is everywhere and not bounded by buildings, the ultimate concept of God in this and other Gnostic literature is that God is pantheistically a part of all things.

At the end of the movie a title scroll says that the "Gospel of St. Thomas has been claimed by scholars around the world to be the closest record we have of the words of the historical Jesus" and that "the Vatican refuses to recognize this gospel and has described it as heresy." Supposedly, the Vatican is ignorantly denying what most scholars have proved.[7]

The fact is, Vatican officials have *not* suppressed the Gospel of Thomas. Nor have they suppressed dozens of other Gnostic texts from Nag Hammadi. All of them are available and have been studied by scholars for years. They were rejected when the canon was formed because they failed to meet the rigorous criteria of Scripture that other books also had to undergo.[8]

Simon Birch, written and directed by Mark Steven Johnson, is a heartwarming coming-of-age story of a little boy named Joe who befriends another little boy with a stunted growth problem named Simon Birch. Simon's disease constantly casts a shadow of death over him. We are told by the grown-up Joe in narration that little Simon is the reason Joe, originally an atheist, now believes in God.

A dominant theme of the movie is that God has a purpose for everyone's life, no matter how small or seemingly unimportant we are. Simon himself repeats the mantra throughout the story, "God has a plan for everyone." Simon tenaciously

Director's Cut

Further reading on the Gospel of Thomas is available at ‹www.godawa.com›.

believes that someday he will be "God's instrument" to "carry out his plan." Just what that plan is, he doesn't know, until unfolding events reveal God's purpose as twofold: first, the inspiration of Joe's belief in God, and second, the event that precipitates that belief (a heroic rescue of little children in a bus accident that leads to Simon's death).

---

[7]According to some responsible scholarship, the Gospel of Thomas was probably a Manichaean tract created sometime around 140 A.D. (years *after* the disciple Thomas died) by a writer who not only depended literarily on the canonical Gospels but also showed clear second-century Gnostic ideas, not yet developed in the time of Christ's disciples (Gregory A. Boyd, *Cynic Sage, or Son of God?* [Grand Rapids, Mich.: Baker, 1995], pp. 133-36). That writer was most likely a disciple of the Gnostic Mani, coincidentally named Thomas (Beate Blatz, "The Coptic Gospel of Thomas," in *New Testament Apocrypha,* ed. Wilhelm Scheenelcher [Louisville, Ky.: Westminster Press, 1991], 1:111-13).

[8]Norman Geisler and William Nix, *A General Introduction to the Bible* (Chicago: Moody Press, 1986), pp. 277-316.

This positive Christian premise is couched in individualistic spiritual-ity. Simon is an outcast not merely because of his runt stature but also because he receives the brunt of the local church's institutional tradition, complete with finger-wagging, tongue-clucking, rule-enforcing uptight-ness. And half the time he is wrongfully accused.

Simon is adamant throughout that he has his own special relationship with God and doesn't need the rules and traditions of church to tell him what to do. He's a rebel with a cause. In a plot twist the "proper" pastor of the church winds up being Joe's mysterious secret birth father from a covered-up adulterous affair. This minister is actually void of real faith himself, also reinforcing the death of institutional authority in religion as mere hypocrisy. Simon pleads with the man of cloth to affirm that God has a plan for everyone—even little Simon—but the minister replies with a lifeless "I can't."

The real difficulty in addressing this issue of individual faith versus institutional faith is that it is a partial truth. The fact is, *there are* negative institutions that oppress the freedom and rights of individuals, as we see in *1984* (1984), *Brazil* (1985), *Dead Poets Society* and *Gattaca* (1997). *There are* dark corridors of power and evil religious leaders. But in focusing exclusively on anti-institutional storytelling and negative authority figures, without a balance of proper authority or submission, movie culture amounts to propaganda that breeds antiauthority bigotry in audiences. As C. S. Lewis wrote, "We make men without chests and expect of them virtue and enterprise. We laugh at honor and are shocked to find traitors in our midst. We castrate and bid the geldings be fruitful."[9]

But not all challenge to authority is wrong. *How* a person brings change is the moral question. Defying rules *without respect or submission* breeds anarchy, with everyone a law unto themselves. Both extremes— oppressive institutions *and* rebellious individuals—are wrong.

One is hard pressed to find a recent film that extols the virtues of accountability to the community. One such film is *White Squall* (1996),

---

[9]C. S. Lewis, *The Abolition of Man* (New York: Macmillan, 1955), p. 35.

adapted by Todd Robinson, depicting a boatload of typical, individualistic young boys who sign up for a sail across the ocean, only to be capsized by a huge wave. Their very survival is dependent upon them following the rules and order laid out by the captain (played by Jeff Bridges) and working together by subordinating their individuality for the greater good of the group. Some military movies, like *Heartbreak Ridge* (1986), *Hanoi Hilton* (1987), *Rules of Engagement* (2000), *Black Hawk Down* (2001) and *We Were Soldiers* (2002), illustrate this team-oriented discipline and subordination of the individual as well.

Doubt Versus Faith

The issue of doubt and faith is not unknown in contemporary cinema. In fact, it's probably the approach most favorable to the postmodern dilemma. By facing doubt, we can sometimes face our own arrogance and discover that we are asking the wrong questions after all. And the internal struggle of the hero trying to discover the truth under his or her own personal crisis is the stuff of great drama.

Shadowlands (1993)—William Nicholson's film adaptation from his play of C. S. Lewis's struggle with love and suffering—is a rather positive portrayal of the Christian life in the face of doubt. It is the love story between Lewis (played by Anthony Hopkins) and Joy Davidman (played by Debra Winger) and her subsequent battle with cancer. Lewis is portrayed as an intellectual who is so absorbed in books and ideas that he lacks the experience of real-life suffering about which he writes so articulately. In fact, he is a bit arrogant because he always wins arguments. In short, he is a know-it-all who has never really experienced loss.

But it is one thing to write clever words of advice and quite another to live them out in flesh and blood. And that is what his journey becomes. The key repeated phrase in the film is "Pain is God's megaphone to a deaf world." And megaphone it is for Lewis as he is surprised by the pain of losing the woman he loves, which leads him to question his faith. This is an honest struggle portrayed with sensitive sympathy as he rediscovers God's severe mercy in the midst of suffering.[10]

Another movie that expresses the goodness and authority of God's will in the face of human doubt is *Commandments* (1997). In this modern retelling of the story of Job, Aidan Quinn plays a young man who suffers just about every loss in life that one can experience. He loses his job, his house, his health and, most precious of all, his wife. He demands an answer from God and doesn't get one, so he embarks upon a quest to break every single one of the Ten Commandments, one by one, until God gives him an answer. He finally gets to the point of suicide, but through miraculous intervention, he is rescued and resigns himself to the fact that God is in control. He finds peace and happiness in a twist of events (reminiscent of those faced by Jonah) ordained by his loving Creator to give his life back to him.

The Third Miracle (1999) is the story of a priest (played by Ed Harris) investigating a series of miracles allegedly performed by a woman who is being considered for sainthood by the Vatican. He is himself a skeptic, but he goes through his own crisis of faith in the process of his work and rediscovers his place in the scheme of things. The Church leaders above him are portrayed ironically as infidels who themselves have no faith amid their headlong pursuit of power.

The End of the Affair (1999)—adapted by Neil Jordan from the novel of the same name by the Roman Catholic Graham Greene—is a story of attempted fidelity to God in the midst of suffering. Set during World War II, this movie presents a successful writer named Maurice who has an adulterous affair with Sarah, his friend's wife. But then one day, after his home is bombed and he has a near-death experience,

---

[10]Unfortunately, even though the film deals with Lewis's faith, it pulls way back from the boldness in the original play, diluting its power. And one tiny line change from the play to the movie stains a potentially great finale. At the end of the film, after Lewis has been humbled in his intellect, he is walking away and we hear his voice-over narrate that he doesn't have "any answers," but he has learned that "the pain now is part of the happiness then—that's the deal." The original line was that he didn't have "all the answers." This subtle difference between "all" and "any" makes all the difference in the world because it transforms his faith from a humble submission to a reasonable God into an existential leap without rational foundation. It seems the filmic Lewis, unlike the real one, went from one wrong extreme to another.

Sarah leaves his life and never tells him why.

Maurice decides to investigate and discovers that she had promised God to stop the adultery if he would save Maurice's life at the bombing. This enrages his atheistic sentiments, and he pursues her until she can no longer remain true to her promise and gives in to his seductions again. But then she gets a terminal illness and on her deathbed repents of it all. This enrages Maurice, who cannot accept a God who wields such power over people's destinies. As he writes a letter of hatred about God, we see the bitter fruit of unbelief in the life of the unrepentant.[11]

The Body

The Body (2001) is worthy of special attention because it brims with every aspect of faith discussed in this and previous chapters: good Christians, bad Christians, insane Christians, blind faith versus proof, individual versus institutional faith, and the battle between doubt and faith.

Antonio Banderas plays Matt, a Jesuit priest who is sent from the Vatican to investigate the alleged discovery of the bones of Jesus Christ in an ancient Jewish grave, found there by Jewish archeologist Sharon (played by Olivia Williams). Needless to say, if these bones are of the Son of Man, this could topple one of the three biggest religions of the world—and you can bet all three have their motives for getting involved.

Vatican officials are intent on suppressing the discovery and are represented as institutional despots. Matt's superior tells him, "We are counting on you to protect the Church." "You mean the faith," replies Matt. "The Church *is* the faith," retorts his superior. Matt asks, "What if this is—" His superior interrupts him by saying, "This is *not* the body of Christ," thus sealing the Catholic leaders as unwilling to face the truth if it contradicts their religious beliefs and as willing to do anything to stop that truth from getting out.

Matt is more genuine and, along with another priest (played by Derek

---

[11]I consider the sex scenes in this otherwise thoughtful film exploitative and therefore a hindrance to its integrity as an examination of the issue of faith and fidelity.

Jacobi), goes through a crisis of faith. The lines of evidence converge to indicate that these are indeed the bones of Christ: rich man's tomb, coins dated from Pilate's reign, crucifixion marks, spear wound on the rib cage, legs unbroken, thornlike damage to the skull. While the older priest commits suicide after going insane because he could not handle the ramifications, Matt suffers psychic torment because, as he says, Jesus is God, so "if you take away the Resurrection, you kill the God, Jesus." He painfully contemplates the conclusion that if Christianity is wrong, then oblivion awaits us when we die.

This is a stunningly biblical truth reiterated by the apostle Paul when he wrote:

> If Christ has not been raised, then our preaching is vain, your faith also is vain. Moreover we are even found to be false witnesses of God, because we testified against God that He raised Christ, whom He did not raise, if in fact the dead are not raised. For if the dead are not raised, not even Christ has been raised; and if Christ has not been raised, your faith is worthless; you are still in your sins. Then those also who have fallen asleep in Christ have perished. If we have hoped in Christ in this life only, we are of all men most to be pitied. (1 Corinthians 15:14-19)[12]

Sharon, in a display of scientific arrogance, tells Matt, "My archeological facts are going to conflict with your religious beliefs."

A Jewish leader wants to use the bones as a bargaining tool with the Vatican for political acknowledgment of the state of Israel. This guy doesn't really care whether it's true or not, because according to his postmodern understanding of faith, he says, "Religion does not exist based on a rational system of proof but because of man's need." He thinks Christian faith will survive because people will still believe contrary to the evidence anyway.

---

[12]No other religion or philosophy makes such a challenge to falsify its authority. Find the bones and you can disprove the faith. Ironically, while these implications are considered by believers, the contrary ones are never examined by unbelievers in such movies, namely that if Christ *is* resurrected and therefore *is* God, then he is the only way to know truth and to find salvation from sin.

Finally, Muslim terrorists want the bones so that they can blackmail both Israel and Christianity to give them their land in Jerusalem.

By the end of the story, Matt discovers the last piece of evidence that proves the bones are a later Christian burial of a man named David and not Christ's own bones.[13] He goes back and quits the Vatican with an inspiring speech of honesty, integrity and *individualistic* faith:

> **I went to prove it was *not* the body of Christ, whether it was true or not. I thought I had lost my faith in Christ my savior, my friend. But I have lost my faith in men like you who serve God for their own material agenda.**

He concludes in a personal-versus-institutional battle for his soul that he will now serve God "in his own way."

Throughout the movie, the concept that "God has no place in politics" is reiterated as the catch phrase for the theme. And this makes one wonder, since the movie proved that God *does* have a place in politics, whether we like it or not. The story seems to indicate that faith is a private thing that should not be brought out into the naked public square, because it results in so much fighting. But this view is itself a particular *political* bias about God's place in politics. It is based on the dogmatic belief that God is only a personal existential experience, a mere belief that

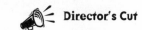 **Director's Cut**

For further reading on the nature of apologetics and the resurrection of Jesus Christ, visit ‹www.godawa.com ›.

---

[13]A dirty little secret of "scientific dating" is revealed in the film when a carbon dating specialist tells Matt that a pot in the tomb is definitely confirmed to be from 70 A.D. But then we learn that she had mistakenly assumed that date from Matt as his suspected "target date." This subtle form of "guided" radioactive dating is an example of the kind of wishful thinking that guides many scientific endeavors. It appears that faith is an inescapable concept even for those most proud of their "empirical objectivity." See Michael A. Cremo and Richard L. Thompson, *Forbidden Archeology: The Hidden History of the Human Race* (San Diego: Bhaktivedanta Institute, 1993), pp. 753-94; see also Martin L. Lubenow, *Bones of Contention: A Creationist Assessment of Human Fossils* (Grand Rapids, Mich.: Baker, 1992), pp. 247-66.

should not be allowed to interact with society in a realistic way.[14]

To Believe or Not to Believe

After considering this sampling review of the nature of faith in film, it should be clear how often spiritual beliefs are worked out through storytelling. For good and bad, movies are a powerful medium for religious expression. Though authentic biblical spirituality is often hard to come by, there is still the kernel of it everywhere, even in the bad Christian movies, anti-Christian movies and movies of angels and Antichrists. Whether it's blind faith versus reasonable faith, individual versus institutional faith or even the confrontation of doubt with faith, filmmakers seem to provide a mixed bag of truth and error when dealing with faith and the human condition.

Watch and Learn

1. Watch a movie about a historical person of faith (such as *Shadowlands* or *Romero,* 1989). How does the movie portray that person's Christian faith? What aspects of faith are ignored or downplayed? What aspects of faith are emphasized? How is the character's faith related to his or her redemption in the story?

2. Watch the movie *Contact.* Compare and contrast how the movie characterizes faith and science. What do you think the movie is saying about the proper relationship of science, faith and society?

---

[14]A rather positive aspect of *The Body* is that the priest never fornicates with the woman, unlike the typical exploitative tactic in stories that explore the relationship of doubt and faith *(The Third Miracle, Simon Birch).*

Conclusion

Watching Movies
with Eyes Wide Open

In this book I have introduced you to the basic structure of storytelling that is used in screenwriting with the intent of sharpening your skills in discerning the worldviews and philosophies that are communicated through Hollywood movies. I then applied those skills to various specific worldviews, including existentialism, postmodernism, monism, Christianity and others, in order to illustrate how trends in thinking and society are reflected in and influenced by movies. Though these principles of discernment are relevant for both adults and youth, many of the examples I have used are from movies that are R-rated or are more adult-oriented. In the same way that we allow alcohol in our culture only for adults who have reached a certain age of maturity, so I think discretion should be used in movies as to the maturity level necessary for a viewer. The

 **Director's Cut**

My website ‹www.godawa.com› includes links to Christian movie review sites.

discerning viewer can consult various previewing sites on the Web to determine the content and detail with which one is comfortable. It is important to remember that not all movies are worthy of our time or attention, because all stories are not created equal.

Discretion and Balance
Just as God permits the adult consumption of wine and strong drink (Deuteronomy 14:26; John 2:1-11) but not its abuse (Ephesians 5:18),

so many movies are for mature viewers because of their content but should not be carelessly consumed without caution or self-reflection as the unwary cultural glutton does. As viewers, we must be sensitive to our own weaknesses and negative propensities. One person's sense of exploitation may simply illustrate his own prudery, while another person's tolerance may actually be her own indulgence in besetting sin. So we must be careful to draw personal lines that we will not cross, based upon what particular things affect us negatively when we are exposed to them in movies.

In the same way that alcoholics won't take a sip of alcohol because they know their weakness toward drunkenness, so adult viewers ought to know their weaknesses and avoid watching those movies or parts of movies that will draw them down spiritually rather than exhort them morally. Statements like "The sex and violence don't bother me" are not necessarily expressions of maturity. If a movie is exploitative with vice, it *ought* to bother the viewer, and if it doesn't, then that viewer is being deadened in his or her spirituality and humanity.

A Love-Hate Relationship

One of the biggest hindrances to valuable discussion of movies is our tendency to "love" or "hate" a movie with such conviction that those who disagree with us are discouraged from communicating or sharing their own viewpoints. If the negative aspects we perceive in a film outweigh the positive aspects, we tend to ignore those positive aspects and reject the movie altogether. If the positive aspects outweigh the negative for us, then we tend to neglect those negatives and wholly endorse the movie with glowing praise. Phrases like "I hated that movie" or "I loved that movie" are often perceived by others as warnings to avoid discussion because of such strong conviction.

Even in writing this book I have struggled with this need for balance. Because of the constraint of space, I have tried to focus on movies that illustrate a particular point, good or bad, without examining counterpoints. One unintended result may be the appearance of unqualified approval or disapproval of a movie. Be careful not to jump to this conclusion. An analysis of a movie does not necessarily mean an *absolute* endorsement or rejection of that movie.

The Good, the Bad and the Mediocre

If my intentions for this book have been successful, you will walk away from the book with a more balanced appreciation for movies, both those you like and those you dislike. You will have the ability to appreciate the good and pinpoint what you think is bad. Movies, after all, are art, and therefore they are meant to stimulate thought and challenge preconceived notions.

Talking about movies seems problematic at times because people take their perceptions so personally. If we love a movie that someone else hates, we tend to think the other is a pessimist and may dislike us as well. If we hate a movie that someone else loves, we tend to think the other may be overly optimistic and blissfully ignorant. And in both cases we wonder how blind the other could be not to have seen what we have seen. Sometimes we even question that person's character. How can we avoid this kind of communication barrier and engage in helpful dialogue about the movies we see?

Persuading Versus Arguing

I have found that the approach most conducive to openness in discussion is describing what I liked about a movie first, even if I "hated" the movie, and then to describe what I didn't like or disagreed with in its craft or content. Whether others hated a movie or loved it, they will be more likely to consider your perspective and welcome dialogue if you have shown a balance of perception and have focused on the positive first. And there's usually *something* good about every film, no matter how bad it is. Sometimes you just have to work harder to find that positive.

Of course this approach can be taken wrongly to an extreme. For instance, the discussion of the acting or directing in a pornographic film does not justify consuming such depravity. Discussing the realism of special effects in a slasher film that exploits the destruction of human bodies amounts to a rationalization as well. Be careful: "All things are lawful for me, but not all things are profitable. . . . I will not be mastered by anything" (1 Corinthians 6:12).

This brings up a common complaint about the mixture of good and bad in movies. Rare is the film that can be fully embraced in all it communicates. Some people believe that since movies are such a mixture of truth and error in their worldviews and values, Christians should avoid watching them for the sake of holy living. They claim that allowing a little bit of "compromise" leads to the slippery slope of more and bigger compromise until one falls away from the faith (or at least falters in one's spiritual walk).

While there is merit in this argument regarding those who would subject themselves to things that they feel draw them away from God, let me redirect our thoughts to the appendix at the back of this book on sex, violence and profanity in the Bible. We must remember that not all exploration of sins within drama is exploitative or inherently sinful. Since the Bible itself explores human evil with great breadth and much detail, we cannot say that movies that do so are, without exception, exploitative. If we do, we run the risk of accusing the original Author of our faith of being exploitative himself.

The key is to ask some questions: Is this an educational approach to exposing evil? What are the context and consequences of the vice portrayed? Is it dehumanizing or humanizing? Does the movie celebrate evil, or does it ultimately condemn it? Is the sin displayed as an end in itself, or is it a part of the bigger picture that leads to redemption? Does the movie go overboard in detail, or is some detail necessary to emphasize the seriousness of our behavior? Only in this way can we avoid the extremes of cultural gluttony and cultural anorexia, which are both detrimental to our humanity as created in the image of God.

And we need not be afraid of being challenged by worldviews that contradict our own. Sometimes elements of our own worldview may not be true and we need to be challenged to reexamine them, even from a viewpoint with which we ultimately disagree. Of course that takes humility.

The fact is, there is nothing perfect in this life. We live in a fallen world. Everything and everyone is tainted by sin, even those with whom we agree. Even Christian media are not exempt from imperfection. No Christian sermon, book or movie is completely unstained by our fallenness. But we do not cut off all contact with Christian culture because of this reality. We interact with it. So we should deal with "secular" culture as well, discerning the truth and error in art that radiate a "fallen splendor."

As Christians, we do not walk away from an unbeliever because he or she cusses or lives in open rebellion against God; we interact with that person in order to find common ground in our humanity and eventually offer redemption for sin. We do not walk out of a sermon that we disagree with; we interact with the preacher afterward to express solidarity with what we agreed with and to try to offer correction where we see error. It is the same with the arts. Because all truth is ultimately God's truth, we can find what we think is truth in a movie and dissect what we think is false. Sometimes the false or the evil becomes too much and we walk out of the theater or fast-forward the video. This is inevitable. But our goal should be to interact with society with a view toward reform, not to retreat from society, for retreat leads to spiritual and social defeat.

The Apostle Paul's Example

In Acts 17 the apostle Paul models a redemptive interaction with culture. He addresses the pagans of his day (the Epicureans and Stoics) within the arena of ideas of his day (the Areopagus). Paul was not afraid of engaging those heathen ideas.

In some ways television, music and the movies are the modern arena of ideas. Many people are influenced in their worldview by the entertainment industry, whether willingly or unwittingly. Like Paul, we had best be informed about the media of communication in our culture.

Paul studied Greek culture and philosophy under Gamaliel (Acts

22:3).[1] He analyzed the religious altars of the Greeks (v. 23) and made himself familiar with their deities so that he could contrast them with "the Lord of heaven and earth, who does not dwell in temples built by human hands" (v. 24). Then he respectfully quoted several Greek poets, including Homer (or Plato, v. 27), Epimenides, Aratus and Cleanthes (v. 28), deconstructing their comments to show that they reflected only a twisted glimpse of God's original truth.[2]

In a quatrain addressing Zeus, Epimenides had written, "In him we live and move and exist"; Zeus was alive because living human beings carried the idea of him within them. Paul reversed the order: we live because God lives. The true God is not dependent on human beings but himself "gives to all life and breath and all things" (v. 25). Paul endorsed Aratus's claim that we are "God's offspring" not in a pantheistic sense but in the sense that God "made from one every nation of mankind to live on all the face of the earth." God is our father in the sense that he is our Creator and we are made in his image. Paul thus brought out of the Greek pagan beliefs a more accurate rendering of the truth by *interacting with* the culture, not by avoiding it or embracing it.[3]

Weighing In on the Weaker Brother

A common reaction to the difficulty of sifting through movies mixed with truth and error is to avoid them altogether on behalf of the "weaker brother" (or sister). When handling the issue of those who consider all

---

[1]"When we add to this the extensive knowledge of Greek literature and culture which is reflected in his letters, it is manifest that Paul was neither naïve nor obscurantist when it came to a knowledge of philosophy and Gentile thought" (Greg Bahnsen, *Always Ready: Directions for Defending the Faith*, ed. Robert Booth [Atlanta: American Vision, 1996], p. 241).

[2]In suggesting that we may "perhaps grope for Him and find Him, though he is not far from each one of us," Paul uses the same word used by Homer of the blind Cyclops vainly reaching for Odysseus and his men, and used by Plato in reference to "amateur guesses at the truth" (ibid., pp. 260-61).

[3]Some might argue that Paul was acquainted with Greek culture *before* he became a Christian. Though this is likely true, Paul's history as a "Hebrew of Hebrews; . . . a Pharisee" (Philippians 3:4) meant that he engaged the surrounding culture while maintaining a devout adherence to the law of God. Apparently he did not consider it a compromise to interact redemptively with his cultural environment.

movies to be worldly or evil, some people make recourse to the places in the New Testament where the apostle Paul deals with those who believed eating meat sacrificed to idols was a violation of spiritual holiness (Romans 14; 1 Corinthians 8). Paul calls these people "weak in faith" because idols are nothing and carry no power or authority over the God who created food to eat.

Even though the one who is stronger in faith is not morally wrong to eat such meat, he or she must be sensitive and curtail consumption *in the presence of* the weaker brother so as not to be a stumbling block. Why? Because for the weaker brother, *who may follow the stronger brother in deference,* the principle of violating his conscience is still sinful. Even though the act itself is not wrong to God, the motivation of doing what one thinks is wrong is nonetheless also wrong.

Certain Christians erroneously conclude that since some "weaker brother" Christians believe movies are wrong, others should not watch movies. Is this a fair and reasonable assumption? The problem is that the person whom most people refer to as a "weaker brother" is in fact not weaker at all but rather a strongly convinced or even pharisaical brother.

Strongly convinced Christians will not stumble by seeing others watching movies, because they won't watch them themselves. They won't go against their conscience. And the Pharisee who condemns those who watch movies will himself never watch a movie because of his own legalistic mindset. We moviegoing faithful are not beholden to these Christians, because *they will not stumble by our actions.* They will not go against their consciences. In fact, they will argue their point vociferously, explaining why they will not do so and why you should not do so as well. To the strongly convinced believers and pharisaical legalists, Paul gives this admonition:

> The one who [watches movies] is not to regard with contempt the one who does not [watch movies], and the one who does not [watch movies] is not to judge the one who [does watch movies], for God has accepted him. Who are you to judge the servant of another? To his own master he stands or falls; and he will stand, for the Lord is able to make him stand. . . . Each

person must be fully convinced in his own mind. . . . But you, why do you judge your brother? Or you again, why do you regard your brother with contempt? For we shall all stand before the judgment seat of God. (Romans 14:3-5, 10, slightly paraphrased)

Contrary to the convinced believer and the Pharisee, the weaker brother is the one who *will* go against his own conscience because of the actions of those who are stronger (1 Corinthians 8:7). This is the brother who, though believing it is wrong to watch movies, sees a stronger brother doing so and, on the basis of his regard for that brother, sets aside his own convictions and imitates the one he respects. This is the one who violates his conscience. And this is the brother whom the strong in faith must take into consideration when they exercise their freedom. The watchers of movies are not required to curtail their consumption of media culture simply because there are Christians around them who disagree with them. To disagree is not be a "weaker brother." To disagree and yet follow another *against one's beliefs* is to be a weaker brother.

Director's Cut

Further reading on Christianity and the arts can be found at ‹www.godawa.com›. A biblical and scholarly approach to questions of the "weaker brother" and Christian liberty can be found in Kenneth L. Gentry Jr., "Bible Teaching on Christian Liberty," chapter six in *God Gave Wine: What the Bible Says About Alcohol* (Lincoln, Calif.: Oakdown, 2001), pp. 105-30.

This difference between the weaker brother and the stronger brother or the Pharisee is reflected in Paul's two opposing commands: "[1] Do not destroy with your food [or movie watching] him for whom Christ died. [2] Therefore do not let what is for you a good thing be spoken of as evil" (Romans 14:15-16). Paul appears to be saying we should not let our freedom bring down the weaker brother and that, at the same time, we should take a stand against the impropriety of legalistic man-made rules.

Simple disagreement is not justification for celluloid abstinence. But we must be sensitive to those who would follow us against their consciences and recognize that it is a serious responsibility with serious consequences if we flaunt our freedom without mature circumspection. "For through your knowledge he who is weak is ruined, the brother for whose sake Christ died. And so, by sinning against the brethren and wounding their conscience when it is weak, you sin against Christ" (1 Corinthians 8:11-12).

Watch and Learn

Invite friends to begin a movie discussion group. Try to pick movies that will be the least offensive for a wider appeal. Watch different kinds of movies each time, like a comedy, a foreign film, an art-house film, a "chick flick," a guy movie, a drama and so on. Have viewers read *Hollywood Worldviews* before they join.

Be a facilitator for the discussion. Ask questions like the following:

1. *The craft:* What did you like and not like about the craft and production of the film? What about the writing, directing, cinematography and acting?

2. *The story:* Whose story is this? What is the character arc and redemption of the hero? Discuss the arc with examples from the movie. What is the hero's inner flaw? What choice does the hero make to overcome the flaw? What is the theme or themes explored in the movie?

3. *The worldview:* What worldviews are explored in the film and how are they honored or dishonored? What do you think the filmmakers are saying about the human condition and how we ought or ought not live?

Appendix

Sex, Violence &
Profanity in the Bible

A dominant theme of cultural critics addressing movies is the preoccupation that many films have with sex, violence and profanity. Many studies have linked media consumption with degenerate social behavior. Statistics show that Americans absorb into their minds thousands of violent acts, vile obscenities and acts of immoral sexuality through the media every year. But the part of the puzzle not typically addressed is the context out of which these sinful acts pour forth. And it is perhaps here that the most damage *or good* can be done to the individual and society.

Although violence and sexual immorality are results of the Fall in Eden, all *accounts* of sex and violence are not intrinsically immoral. It is the context through which these misbehaviors are communicated that dictates their destructive or redemptive nature. It is not merely the detailed acts of violence portrayed in teen slasher series like *Friday the 13th, Scream* or *Nightmare on Elm Street* that make them detrimental to the minds of youth. It is that these acts exist within a nihilistic view of the world as survival of the fittest, with murder demythologized through diabolical detail and the existential association of sex with death. The devaluing of human life is realized through evil as entertainment. On the other hand, films like *Schindler's List, Braveheart* and *Saving Private Ryan* portray equally graphic brutality, but their context is ultimately redemptive. That is, the depiction of man's inhumanity toward man points toward righteous resistance and ultimate redemption from such evil. Similar extremities of violence can issue from different contexts and produce opposite results.

The Good Book and Bad Deeds

The ultimate source book for most media watchdogs is the Bible. And it ought to be, because without its definition of a universal objective morality, we have no absolute reference point for right and wrong. Without God's definitions of good and evil, there can be no ultimate value difference between the diabolical acts of Hannibal Lecter and the innocent ones of Forrest Gump. The Bible alone provides a justifiable objective standard for making moral judgments that transcend the whims of personal opinion.

But we must be careful in our appeal to the Good Book when analyzing the morality of stories. For in its pages are detailed accounts and descriptions of every immoral act known to humanity. A cursory perusal of these depictions of vice is enough to make any concerned reader blush. But it only proves that sex and violence are not always literary taboo in Holy Writ. In fact, the acknowledgment of evil is treated as the necessary prerequisite to redemption.

An Example of Violence

Let's take a look at the following interesting passage from a script and examine it in light of moral scruples. The first is a scene from a period piece that takes place in a distant exotic land. Ehud, our swashbuckling hero, is about to give a "message" to the evil villain, King Eglon, who is oppressing Ehud's people like some kind of Darth Vader:

> Ehud made himself a sword which had two edges, a cubit in length, and he bound it on his right thigh under his cloak. He presented the tribute to Eglon king of Moab. Now Eglon was a very fat man. . . . And all who attended [Eglon] left him. Ehud came to him while he was sitting alone in his cool roof chamber. And Ehud said, "I have a message from God for you." And he arose from his seat. And Ehud stretched out his left hand, took the sword from his right thigh and thrust it into his belly. The handle

also went in after the blade, and the fat closed over the blade, for he did not draw the sword out of his belly; and the refuse came out. Then Ehud went out into the vestibule and shut the doors of the roof chamber behind him, and locked them.

When he had gone out, his servants came and looked, and behold, the doors of the roof chamber were locked; and they said, "He is only relieving himself in the cool room." They waited until they became anxious; but behold, he did not open the doors of the roof chamber. Therefore they took the key and opened them, and behold, their master had fallen to the floor dead.

Now Ehud escaped while they were delaying, and he passed by the idols and escaped to Seirah.

What script is this from? An Arnold Schwarzenegger action movie? The next installment of *Terminator?* Obviously not. The informed reader already knows this is a passage from the Bible—Judges 3:16-26, to be precise. God, as the sovereign author of human history, wrote this script, and it's loaded with lies, espionage, intrigue, murder and a rather grotesque image of a man's bowels spilling out over a plunged weapon. And it all ends with an escape scene reminiscent of many action films today. I could go on, but you get the picture. Parental discretion advised.

Examples of Sex

How about this steamy sex scene dialogue?

How beautiful are your feet in sandals,
O prince's daughter!
The curves of your hips are like jewels,
The work of the hands of an artist.
Your navel is like a round goblet
Which never lacks mixed wine;
Your belly is like a heap of wheat
Fenced about with lilies.
Your two breasts are like two fawns,

Sex

Adultery (Judges 19:22-25; 1 Samuel 2:22; 2 Samuel 11; Proverbs 2; 5; 7)

Incest (Genesis 11:29; 19:31-36; 35:22; 38:16-18)

Masochism and satanic worship (1 Kings 18:25-28)

Orgies (Exodus 32:3-6)

Prostitution (Genesis 38:12-26; Judges 16:1)

Rape—even gang rape (Genesis 34:2; Judges 19:22-25; 2 Samuel 13:6-14)

Seduction (Proverbs 7)

Violence

Annihilation of entire cities (Genesis 19:23; Joshua 6:21; 8:22-26; 10:34-42)

Bludgeoning of a thousand men to death (Judges 15:15-16)

Burning victims alive (Numbers 16:35; Joshua 7:25; Judges 9:49; 15:6; Daniel 3:22)

Cannibalism (2 Kings 6:28)

Cutting off of thumbs (Judges 1:6-7)

Decapitation (1 Samuel 17:5; 31:9; 2 Samuel 16:9)

Disemboweling (Judges 3:21-22; 2 Samuel 20:10; 2 Chronicles 21:19; Acts 1:18)

Dismemberment (1 Samuel 15:32-33)

Genocide (1 Samuel 22:19; Numbers 31:17; Deuteronomy 2:34; 3:6; Joshua; Matthew 2:16)

Gouging out of eyes (Judges 16:21)

Hanging (Joshua 10:26-27; Esther 9:25; Matthew 27:3-5)

Human sacrifice (2 Kings 3:27; 16:3; 17:17, 31; 21:6; 2 Chronicles 28:3)

Murder after murder after murder (Genesis to Revelation)

Stabbing (Judges 3:16-26; 2 Samuel 2:23; 3:27; 20:10)

Stoning (Numbers 15:36; Joshua 7:25; 1 Kings 21:13; Acts 7:54-59; 14:19)

Striking between the eyes (1 Samuel 17:49)

Suicide (1 Samuel 31:4-5; 2 Samuel 17:23; 1 Kings 16:18; Acts 1:18)

Lawlessness

Arson (Numbers 11:1; Judges 9:49; 15:5; 18:27; 20:48; 2 Kings 25:9)

Blasphemy (Exodus 32:4; 2 Kings 18:4, 28—19:5; Job 2:9; Isaiah 36:14-20)

Destruction of public property (Joshua 6:34; 8:19; 11:11; Judges 1:8; 16:30-31)

Revenge (Genesis 34:25; Judges 15:7-8; 2 Samuel 3:27; 13:23-29; Mark 6:19-24)

Theft (Genesis 31:19, 34-35; Joshua 7:11; Judges 17:2; 18:14-27; John 12:6)

Voyeurism (2 Samuel 11:2)

Vulgar insults (1 Kings 12:10; Galatians 5:12)

Figure 3. Sex, violence and lawlessness depicted in the Bible

Twins of a gazelle. . . .
Your stature is like a palm tree,
And your breasts are like its clusters.
I said, "I will climb the palm tree,
I will take hold of its fruit stalks."
Oh, may your breasts be like clusters of the vine,
And the fragrance of your breath like apples,
And your mouth like the best wine!

Is this some description of Sharon Stone or Elizabeth Hurley in a sexy thriller? On the contrary, it's from the Song of Solomon 7:1-3, 7-9.

And Solomon does not merely dwell on married love in his portraits of sexuality in Scripture. He also pictures a vividly sensual scene of adulterous seduction in Proverbs 7, complete with the detailed smells, sights and sounds of the moment: sensually exotic linens on the bed, sweet-smelling perfume, lustful whispers of enticement. It's enough to make a reader's erotic imagination spin wild. Solomon does this in order to lead the reader vicariously into a realistic experience of the surprise that occurs when the adulteress's apparently sweet bed of "myrrh, aloes and cinnamon" turns out to be in reality an entranceway to the "chambers of death."

The conservative scholars of the *Dictionary of Biblical Imagery* are direct in pointing out translations appropriate for some Song of Solomon passages. Not only do they explain that the image of the "garden" used in Proverbs 5:15-19 and Song of Solomon 4:12-15 is a reference to the woman's sexual organ, but they also clarify one of the "tamed" English translations of Song of Solomon 5:4-5 with a more accurate rendering, true to the double entendre inherent in the original Hebrew. The language refers to a man arousing his wife's genitals:

My lover thrust his hand through the hole,
and my vagina was inflamed,
I arose and opened for my lover.[1]

---

[1]Leland Ryken, James C Wilhoit and Tremper Longman III, eds., *Dictionary of Biblical Imagery* (Downers Grove, Ill.: InterVarsity Press, 1998), p. 777.

And they are not one-sided in their exegesis of sexuality. Regarding Song of Solomon 5:14, they point out:

> In the midst of the one descriptive song of the man, the woman says,
> His arms are rods of gold
>   set with chrysolite.
> His body is like polished ivory
>   decorated with sapphires. (Song of Solomon 5:14 NIV)

> Once again the English translations are reticent and here intentionally obscure the more explicit Hebrew text. It is not his body that is like a slab of ivory, but rather his sexual organ, which is like a tusk of ivory.[2]

Some preach that Christians should not go to R-rated movies. But according to the same prohibitions of those well-meaning preachers, their congregations shouldn't read much of the Bible either. Perhaps this double standard is why sermons on the Song of Solomon are rare to nonexistent in many churches. And the difficulty of depicting *appropriate* sexuality in a sex-saturated culture may explain why the Christian church is hesitant in contributing a positive theology of proper "erotic art" as an alternative to the carnal indulgence of the world.[3] Nevertheless, while biblical passages like the ones discussed above do not justify pornography or obscene entertainment, their erotic visual stimulation, verbal seduction and physical consummation could argu-

---

[2]Ibid., p. 778.

[3]John Stuart Peck, a Greek and Hebrew scholar, as well as a producing artistic director of an Ontario theater company, writes of the need for Christians to produce erotic art that is acceptable to God. By "erotic," he means having artistic fidelity to biblical sexuality, as opposed to pornography. Regarding the Song of Solomon, the biblical example of such eroticism, he says, "If we look at that book, we have to admit that in the Scriptures themselves there is artwork about sex, and, furthermore, there are points in chapters 4 and 7 that are so potentially explicit that most translations muff them. Nevertheless, we would not call these passages pornographic or obscene. We could call them 'erotic.' " John Peck, "Sex in Art—An Erotic Christian Imagination?" *Cornerstone* 30, no. 121 (2001): 15. The article is an edited and enhanced version of a speech he delivered in November 1998 at Regent University, Virginia. The text of that speech can be found at <www.regent.edu/acad/schcom/csfc/journal/peck.html>.

ably warrant the label "Under seventeen not admitted unless accompanied by an adult."

Examples of Profanity

What about vulgar language? Does the Bible contain foul-mouthed dialogue like that found in the movies? Is there any place at all for recounting the profanities that spew from the lips of depraved human beings? The answer may be upsetting to some—profanity actually has its place in the Holy Scriptures.[4]

In 1 Kings 12 the irresponsible King Rehoboam is approached by the people of Israel, who ask for a lighter yoke to bear than the one Rehoboam's father gave them. Rehoboam avoids wise elderly counsel and tells the people by way of analogy, "My little finger is thicker than my father's loins! Whereas my father loaded you with a heavy yoke, I will add to your yoke" (verses 10-11).

Now there are two meanings to this statement. First of all, the Hebrew word for "loins" *(motnayim)* is usually a reference to the middle part of the man's body as his seat of strength. Thus, Rehoboam is more than likely referring to the nature of bodily weakness under a heavier yoke. Solomon's burden on the people was nothing compared to what Rehoboam is going to give them.

However, *motnayim* has in some places been used as a reference to the male generative organ.[5] The language of the Bible is filled with alliterative wordplays and poetic analogies. With this context in mind, Rehoboam appears to be making a double entendre with the pinkie and the penis—a common male insult of powerlessness since the beginning of time (especially from the likes of the "young men" with whom Rehoboam counseled). Even if one considers the "safe" English translation of the word as "loins," the harshness of the insult is no less clear.

---

[4] I am using the dictionary definition for *profanity* as meaning "abusive, vulgar, or irreverent language" *(American Heritage Dictionary,* 3rd ed.).

[5] R. Laird Harris, Gleason L. Archer, Bruce K. Waltke, eds., *Theological Wordbook of the Old Testament* (Chicago: Moody Press, 1980), 1:536-537.

Here, as elsewhere, the Scriptures are not gender-exclusive in their revelation of coarse or derogatory language used by sinners. As the *Dictionary of Biblical Imagery* reveals, "Crude metonymy for women as sexual objects appear in Judges 5:30 (the NIV translates, 'girl,' but the Hebrew is coarse slang; cf. Ecclesiastes 2:8, where women are referred to as 'breasts')."[6]

But there is even more explicit vulgar language elsewhere from the pen of Paul the apostle. In the book of Galatians, Paul is criticizing the Judaizers who sought to enforce circumcision as a necessity for the justification of the believer. These legalists sought to put Gentiles under the yoke of Jewish ceremonial law that had already been abrogated by Christ's death (Ephesians 2:11-16). In short, the Judaizers were teaching that Gentiles had to be circumcised to be saved. This was so serious an issue with the apostle that he used the strongest language possible to negate it: "You have been severed from Christ, you who are seeking to be justified by law" (Galatians 5:4). He uses the very notion of "severing" used in circumcision as a wordplay on their own spiritual condition.

Director's Cut

Visit my website ‹www.godawa.com› for my online essay "Sarcasm in the Bible."

But here's the plot twist: In order to express God's animosity toward those of the "false circumcision," Paul says, "I wish that those who are troubling you would even mutilate themselves" (Galatians 5:12). The Greek word for "mutilate" here is *apokopto,* which means "to cut off."[7] This is a nice English translation of saying, "I wish they would just go all the way and cut off their penises." This harsh dialogue not only uses vulgarity to make a point, but it also carries a mocking tone to it. It's a case of employing coarse sarcasm to express a deadly truth.

---

[6]Ryken, Wilhoit and Longman, *Dictionary of Biblical Imagery,* p. 778. The Hebrew word for "many concubines" used in Ecclesiastes 2:8 is *shiddah,* which translates as "many breasts."

[7]Robert L. Thomas, ed., *New American Standard Exhaustive Concordance of the Bible* (Nashville: Holman, 1981), p. 1634.

Examples of Blasphemy

For those who accept some bad language or cursing in movies as fidelity to reality, a common exception is the use of the Lord's name in vain, or blasphemy. They reason that violation of the Third Commandment is not an acceptable sin to portray.

While this sentiment is certainly respectable in its intent to elevate God's holiness, it is nonetheless inconsistent and unbiblical. What scriptural criterion allows the depiction of every other sin except this one? As a matter of fact, *blasphemy* is defined as "impious, and irreverent speech against God. . . . Blasphemy is always in word or deed, injury, dishonor and defiance offered to God."[8] So, in effect, biblical incidents such as the golden-calf debacle (Exodus 32), the brazen serpent scandal (2 Kings 18:4) and the Baal prophets' contest with Elijah (1 Kings 18:20-39) were acts of blasphemy. Yet these incidents and others like them are described explicitly in the Bible.

Blasphemous speech is a foul smell in the nostrils of God and is therefore deserving of wrath, but *no more wrath than any other sin.* And therefore there is all the more reason to depict it in a truthful light. That's exactly what the Bible does when it records blasphemies from the tongues of men and angels.

We need not look far to uncover the first blasphemy recorded in the Bible, as the serpent prods Eve to defy God: "You surely will not die! For God knows that in the day you eat from it your eyes will be opened, and you will be like God, knowing good and evil" (Genesis 3:4-6). This bald accusation that God is childishly selfish and jealous of humanity's potential is pure blasphemous defiance.

Another example betrays blasphemous self-deification. The king of Babylon muses to himself:

I will ascend to heaven;
I will raise my throne above the stars of God,

---

[8]T. Ress, "Blasphemy," in *International Standard Bible Encyclopedia,* ed. James Orr (Rio, Wis.: Ages Software, version 8.0, 2000), p. 457.

And I will sit on the mount of assembly
In the recesses of the north.
I will ascend above the heights of the clouds;
I will make myself like the Most High. (Isaiah 14:13-14)

Here, Isaiah reveals and records the thoughts of a mere man (or perhaps Satan) blasphemously boasting of making himself like God.

And there are other famous recorded instances of blasphemy in the Scriptures: Job's wife pleading with her husband to "curse God and die" (Job 2:9); King Sennacherib calling Yahweh an impotent, lying deity (Isaiah 36:14-20); Peter denying Christ (Matthew 26:74); the spectators at the cross taunting Jesus (Matthew 27:40); and those who, as quoted by Paul, were saying, "Jesus is accursed" (1 Corinthians 12:3).

Vice and Jesus

When confronted with this plethora of sex and violence, one may be tempted to justify it by an appeal to its journalistic style of reporting history. Historical documentation of sex and violence is not the same as fictional stories containing sex and violence, is it? Well, let's ask Jesus.

In his parables Jesus used fictional accounts of beatings, murder, dismemberment and torture as metaphors and images of the kingdom of God.

And who can ignore the virtual feast of gore and brutality depicted in the book of Revelation? In this imaginative vision given to John *by Jesus himself,* we are swept along with special effects that outdo those of George Lucas's Industrial Light and Magic and with horror imagery that makes Stephen King nightmares look like children's bedtime stories. (Incidentally, King and other horrormeisters draw a good portion of their fantastical imagination from Judeo-Christian spiritual imagery.) No matter what end-times school of thought they adhere to in interpreting the book of Revelation, one thing is agreed upon by most Bible students: prophetic literature communicates eternal truth through violent images of imagination and metaphor.

Scripture	Parable	Fictional Sins Described
Matthew 22:1-13	The king's wedding feast	Beatings, murder, war, arson
Matthew 18:23-35	The unforgiving servant	Choking, torture in prison
Matthew 24:45-51	The faithful and unfaithful slaves	Beatings, drunken parties, *Hannibal*-like bodily dismemberment
Matthew 18:6	Millstone metaphor	*Godfather*-style drowning
Matthew 18:7-9	Analogy of sin's seriousness	Gouging out of eyes, cutting off of hands (reminiscent of *Seven*)
Matthew 7:24-26	House built on sand	Destruction of private property

Figure 4. Parables and metaphors of Jesus that protray sinful behavior

Revelation	Imagery
9:1-11	Genetically mutated monsters chasing and tormenting screaming people
9:13-18	Armies of bizarre beasts wreaking death and destruction on the masses
12:3-4	A demonic dragon chasing a woman with the intent to eat her infant child
11:7-13	A beast dragging rotting corpses through the streets for three days while people party over them
19:17-18	Birds eating human and animal remains
17:1-5	A harlot having sex with kings and merchants
20:13-14	Dead people being reanimated and thrown alive into a lake of fire to be tormented forever

Figure 5. Violent imagery in Revelation

Explicit Drama and Allegory in the Old Testament

God often used socially uncomfortable drama as a means of communicating truths to people. He commanded Hosea to marry a prostitute named Gomer in order to embody the nature of Israel's faithless relationship to her spiritual husband, God (Hosea 1). He commanded Isaiah to walk around naked for three years to emphatically declare the shame of what would happen to the Egyptians and Ethiopians (Isaiah 20:2-4).[9] In effect, God used prostitution and naked performance art to make his point!

Explicit sexual immorality appears to be one of God's favorite dramatic metaphors for spiritual apostasy, because he used it so frequently to exclaim derogatory insults against Israel (Exodus 34:15-16; Leviticus 17:7; Deuteronomy 31:16; Judges 2:17; Isaiah 50:1; 54; Jeremiah 3:2-8; Ezekiel 16; 23; Hosea 1:2; 9:1). God even goes so far as to pictorialize his punishment of Israel in the shockingly graphic terms of gang rape:

> O harlot, hear the word of the LORD. Thus says the Lord GOD, . . . "I will gather all your lovers with whom you took pleasure, even all those whom you loved and all those whom you hated. So I will gather them against you from every direction and expose your nakedness to them. . . . I will also give you into the hands of your lovers, and they will . . . strip you of your clothing, take away your jewels, and will leave you naked and bare. They will incite a crowd against you and they will stone you and cut you to pieces with their swords. They will burn your houses with fire and execute judgments on you in the sight of many women. Then I will stop you from playing the harlot, and you will also no longer pay your lovers." (Ezekiel 16:35-41)

In Isaiah 47:1-3, Jeremiah 13:22, Hosea 2:3 and Nahum 3:5-6 God uses the metaphor of "stripping naked" and "lifting the skirt" to inspire shame, with the added indecency, in the Nahum passage, of pelting a body with excrement as a lucid metaphor of punishment for spiritual whoredom.

---

[9]Some scholars question whether this nakedness is stark or modestly limited. It is possible that the command to Isaiah to take off his sackcloth did not necessarily entail removing his tunic underneath (his underwear). Conservative commentators Keil and Delitzsch say, "With the great importance attached to the clothing in the East, where the feelings upon this point are peculiarly sensitive and modest, a person was looked upon as stripped and naked if he had only taken off his upper garment. What Isaiah was directed to do, therefore, was simply opposed to common custom, and not to moral decency." C. F. Keil and F. Delitzsch, *Isaiah*, Commentary on the Old Testament (Albany, Ore.: AGES Software, Version 1.0, 1997), 7:294. But even granting this conservative interpretation, we see that he nonetheless violated the social customs of modesty.

In Ezekiel 23 the prostitution allegory of spiritual apostasy is taken to the limit and elucidated with scandalously immodest description: "She [Samaria] was a prostitute in Egypt. There she lusted after her lovers, whose genitals were like those of donkeys and whose emission was like that of horses. So you longed for the lewdness of your youth, when in Egypt your bosom was caressed and your young breasts fondled" (Ezekiel 23:19-21).

Shocking metaphor and explicit drama are common means by which God communicates to people when they have become thick-skulled, dull of hearing or wicked of heart. One might say, with tongue firmly planted in cheek, that God was the original Shakespeare.

The True, the Honorable and the Pure

"Finally, brethren, whatever is true, whatever is honorable, whatever is right, whatever is pure, whatever is lovely, whatever is of good repute, if there is any excellence and if anything worthy of praise, dwell on these things" (Philippians 4:8). Readers of Bible passages like this one often misunderstand the language to be expressing a "hear no evil, see no evil, speak no evil" approach to spirituality. But ignoring the dark side is not at all what the verses are indicating.

It is not only true that Jesus is the way, the truth and the life, but it is also true that Satan is the father of lies (John 8:44) and that false prophets are his minions (2 Corinthians 11:14-15). It is not only true, honorable and right that Noah was depicted in the Bible as a righteous man, but it is also true, honorable and right that all the rest of the earth around him were depicted as entirely wicked (Genesis 6:5). It is not only profitable to us that Lot was revealed as a righteous man, but it is also profitable that the inhabitants of Sodom were revealed as unprincipled men "who indulge[d] the flesh in its corrupt desires and despise[d] authority" (2 Peter 2:10).

If we ignore truth's darker side, we are focusing on half-truths, and there are no better lies than half-truths. Think of it this way: Is it not honorable, right and pure that God drowned every person on the earth except for eight people (Genesis 8)? Is it not honorable, right and pure that God destroyed Sodom and Gomorrah and all their immoral inhabitants with fire and brimstone (2 Peter 2:6-9)? Is it not lovely, good and excellent that God had the Israelites kill every man, woman and child of the Canaanites with the edge of the sword (Joshua 6:21; 10:30, 37, 39)? To answer no to any of these questions is to ascribe dishonor, wrongness, impurity and unlovely behavior to God himself. The implication is unavoidable: the depiction of evil *and its destructive ends* can be just as true, honorable, right, pure, lovely, excellent, worthy of praise and profitable as can the depiction of righteousness and its glorious ends.

We must face the fact that the Scriptures depict sinful acts that are revolting to our sensibilities. The portrayal of good and the portrayal of evil are two sides of God's revelation to us of his one good and holy truth. This is *not* to say that God himself has a dualistic light side and dark side to his nature, or even that good cannot exist apart from evil, but rather that God has chosen to include depictions of both evil and good in his revelation of truth to us. So pointing out wrong is part of dwelling on what is right, exposing lies is part of dwelling on the truth, revealing cowardice is part of dwelling on the honorable, and uncovering corruption is part of dwelling on the pure.

Speaking of Things Done in Secret

Another concern that some Christians have with the cinematic depiction of deeds of the flesh is that it violates Paul's admonition that "it is disgraceful even to speak of the things which are done by [the sons of disobedience] in secret" (Ephesians 5:12). They read this to mean that we should not even *talk* about the evil that people do, let alone *watch* acts of depravity displayed before our eyes in movies. After all, David declared,

I will set no worthless [evil or unprofitable][10] thing before my eyes;

---

[10]In Hebrew the word translated "worthless" is *bel-e-yah'-al* ("worthless"). Francis Brown, S. R. Driver, Charles Briggs, and William Gesenius, eds., *Hebrew-Aramaic-English Lexicon* (Online Bible, version 3.01, 2001).

> I hate the work of those who fall away;
> It shall not fasten its grip on me. (Psalm 101:3)

I believe this viewpoint misunderstands the text. In fact, a closer examination of the context of Ephesians 5 will reveal that Paul is saying the exact opposite!

Look at the verses before and after this "disgraceful to speak" verse. Ephesians 5:11: "Do not participate in the unfruitful deeds of darkness, but instead even expose them." Ephesians 5:13: "But all things become visible when they are exposed by the light, for everything that becomes visible is light."

Paul is not telling us to *avoid* talking about deeds of darkness because of their disgracefulness; rather, he is telling us to *expose* them by talking about them! By bringing that which is disgracefully hidden out into the light, we show it for what it really is. It is precisely because many sins are disgraceful that they are done in secret, so dealing openly with them exposes them as such, and this aids us in the pursuit of godliness.

Exploitation and Exhortation

Now, what is to be made of all this sex and violence permeating the defining moral standard of Western civilization, the Bible? Is this hypocrisy or self-contradiction? Does such ribald revelation of humanity's darker side in Scripture justify exploitation of our prurient baser instincts? Are Christians defenseless against unbelievers who claim the Bible is X-rated and compare it to pornography? May it never be! Having laid down a rationale for the depiction of depravity, let us now qualify that rationale with *context, context, context*. And context makes all the difference between moral *exhortation* and immoral *exploitation* of sin.

Exploitation, in this context, is the unethical or selfish use of something. Exploitation in movies would amount to an unethical use of sex or violence unintended by Scripture. But what is the intent and extent of Scripture's use of sex and violence? In all of the impropriety portrayed in the Bible we see several elements that make it very different in nature from the lurid celebration of wickedness seen in exploitative movies.

1. Intent. Most biblical spectacle is not exploitative in its intent. It is historical reporting on the highest ground. The storyteller cannot stop the evil that people do, but he can use that evil against them through eyewitness testimony. The writers *expose* man's inhumanity against man for the purpose of moral instruction and with the intent of avoiding the doomed repetition of history.

This is the kind of storytelling involved in such movies as *Schindler's List* (1993), *Braveheart* (1995), *Rob Roy* (1995) and *Amistad* (1997). But it is also found in fictional stories aspiring to be true to the time period, like *Dances with Wolves* (1990), *Last of the Mohicans* (1992), *Saving Private Ryan* (1998), *The Patriot* (2000) or *Gladiator* (2000). Those viewers who would have trouble sitting through such pictures would probably have similar problems reading through the gory details of such biblical books as Judges or Joshua.

2. Depiction. True, evil is depicted in the Scripture, but not through intimate detail or excessive indulgence. Humankind's depravity is not emphasized more than our redemptive potential. Sin is a manifestation of the need for redemption, not an object of obsessive focus.

While the biblical text does not avoid divulging David's adultery with Bathsheba or Shechem's rape of Dinah, it *does* avoid voyeuristic explorations of body crevices and private parts writhing in sexual ecstasy or pain. When David cuts off Goliath's head, we are not indulged in a slow-motion close-up of the sword piercing the neck and the carotid artery spurting blood as the eyes pop and the flesh rips. This kind of violence may arguably be described as pornographic.

Of course, the nature of literature allows mystery and room for the imagination that avoids exploitation, and this allowance is not as easily achieved with the visual medium of cinema. But it can be done. Remember the fade-out that used to always follow the kiss? Alfred Hitchcock was famous for his suspenseful moral tales devoid of cinematic gore, and they are still among the finest films to watch. Narrative summary is the main technique that biblical writers use to avoid indulgence in the titillation of sin while addressing it honestly, and it remains for contemporary film-makers to find new ways to break through the all-too-common exploita-tion of sex and violence with new means of subtlety and diversion.

As a qualifying note, there can be value to showing certain details of depravity if it is done appropriately. As indicated in the Judges pas-sage above, there are some detailed descriptions in the Bible that turn the stomach. In the same way, the horrors of war simply could not be captured in the twenty-minute scene of Omaha Beach in *Saving Pri-vate Ryan* (1998) without showing the effects on bodies of military weaponry.

Jurassic Park (1993) is a powerful tale of the danger of technological progress without moral restraint—a common theme of science fiction and horror. If we follow the foolhardy maxims of some scientists who say, "If it can be done, it should be done," we will end up creating some-thing that will destroy us. The ferocity of the dinosaurs is necessary to embody that moral.

On the other hand, another movie with a similar message, the remake of *Night of the Living Dead* (1990), just like its original (1968), defeats its own moral warning against unrestrained science by exploiting to an obscene extent the detail of zombies eating human flesh and being muti-lated by the heroes. The line for acceptable portrayal of evil must be drawn by the adult individual somewhere between the two extremes of dishonest avoidance of all iniquity and gluttonous imbibing in unneces-sary detail of sex or violence.

3. Consequences. In the Bible sinful behavior always has conse-quences. Sin leads to destruction, not to freedom unfettered by moral restraint. In Genesis, Jacob's deception leads to paranoia and backfires against him. The sins committed in Sodom and Gomorrah lead to fire and brimstone. David's adultery leads to the loss of a son. All this is a far cry from the manipulative attempts of movies like *The Age of Innocence* (1993), *Philadelphia* (1993), *And the Band Played On* (1993), *The Scar-let Letter* (1995), *The People Versus Larry Flint* (1996), *The Crucible* (1996), *Wilde* (1997), *American Beauty* (1999), *Boys Don't Cry* (1999),

Quills (2000) and *Chocolat* (2000) to legitimize destructive sexual behavior and portray their deviants as poor victims of puritanical oppression.[11] But other movies, like *Fatal Attraction* (1987), *Damage* (1992), *Anna Karenina* (1997), *The End of the Affair* (1999), *The Talented Mr. Ripley* (1999) and *Eyes Wide Shut* (1999), explore alternate death styles with more truthful negative consequences.

Fight Club—a movie that on its surface appears to be an excursion into violence as a way of solving life's problems—is actually a moral fable about the negative consequences of pursuing that line of thinking. As the main character gets deeper into his friendship with a reckless man who lives dangerously, he soon discovers that the reckless man is merely a projection of his own dark side that is leading him to destruction, and the main character must stop him before he takes his depravity to its logical conclusion.

This kind of moral teaching by way of the negative (via negativa) is also the purpose of tragedies. Traditionally, tragedies contain sad endings, rather than happy endings, not because they are trying to communicate despair but because they are trying to exhort us as to the consequences of certain common flaws in human nature. The tragic flaw in the hero, such as ambition *(Macbeth)*, jealousy *(O)*, greed *(Wall Street)*, wrath *(Seven)* or glory *(Amadeus)*, is the cause of his downfall, thus illustrating the wages of sin and inspiring the viewers to live contrarily.

The danger, however, of focusing too exclusively on the wages of sin can lead to the very exploitation of sin that the story is trying to critique. *Natural Born Killers* (1994, written by David Veloz, Richard Rutowski and Oliver Stone, from an original story by Quentin Tarantino) tries to capture America's fascination with violence and criminal celebrities, but it runs

---

[11]An increasing occurrence in more recent movies is portrayal of the homosexual as a wise mentor or sympathetic sidekick who has the most humane life and a better understanding of love and romance than do heterosexuals. *The Adventures of Priscilla, Queen of the Desert* (1994), *The Birdcage* (1996), *As Good As It Gets* (1997), *My Best Friend's Wedding* (1997), *Chasing Amy* (1997), *The Love Letter* (1999), *Flawless* (1999), *Bounce* (2000), *The Next Best Thing* (2000), *The Mexican* (2001), *American Beauty* (1999), *Bridget Jones' Diary* (2001), *Billy Elliot* (2001) and other films engage in this or similar attempts to normalize homosexuality.

perilously close to being a celebration of violence and depravity itself, with its MTV-style hipness and its commingling of humor with cruelty.

4. Context. Immoral deeds in the Bible are always contextually presented as immoral. As already pointed out above, evil is not glamorized as entertainment and sin is not presented as an "alternate lifestyle." There is always a call to redemption, the hope for a better humanity, not the nihilistic negation of "This is real life, baby. Get used to it." There is no sense of catharsis, the rationalization of purging evil through acting it out that is sometimes used by artists to justify excessive brutality and evil in films. Noted film director Martin Scorsese has disclosed such dark intentions: "Maybe we need the catharsis of bloodletting and decapitation like the ancient Romans needed it, as ritual but not real like the Roman circuses."[12]

Gory teen slashers and horror movies *(Scream,* 1996; *I Know What You Did Last Summer,* 1997; *From Dusk Till Dawn,* 1996; *John Carpenter's Vampires,* 1998) are not the only films that can fall into the category of cathartic saturation in blood. Many "shoot-'em-up" action movies can degenerate into dehumanization. Some action movies push the envelope in their pursuit of justice and personal redemption by focusing too heavily on finding new ways people can be beat up, shot up or carved up, resulting in what some argue is exploitation (consider *Robocop,* 1987; *Terminator 2,* 1991; *Last Man Standing,* 1996; *3000 Miles to Graceland,* 2001). Revenge movies that have their heroes satisfy their sense of justice outside of the law or through vigilante means without moral repercussions could

 **Director's Cut**

For an online essay on justice in *A Time to Kill* and other movies, see "A Time for Revenge? Vigilantism and Movie Justice in *A Time to Kill*" at ‹www.godawa.com›.

also arguably be called exploitation (consider *The Crow,* 1994; *A Time to Kill,* 1996; *L.A. Confidential,* 1997; *Get Carter,* 2000; *In the Bedroom,* 2001), as could movies that portray villainous or criminal characters as

---

[12]Quoted in Michael Medved, *Hollywood Versus America* (New York: HarperCollins, 1992), p. 199.

heroic or victorious (consider *The Newton Boys,* 1998; *Lock, Stock and Two Smoking Barrels,* 1998; *Hannibal,* 2000; *Gone in Sixty Seconds,* 2000; *Swordfish, American Outlaws, Bandits, Heist, The Score, Ocean's Eleven,* all 2001).

But be careful. Just because a villain gets away doesn't always mean the story is glorifying villains or saying that crime pays. Sometimes, as in *The Usual Suspects* (1995), *Primal Fear* (1996) or *American Psycho* (2000), it is a broader moral statement of warning. These stories are cautionary tales that warn us of the deceiving nature of evil and of how we can be duped if we are not careful.

In *Primal Fear,* written by Steve Shagan and Ann Biderman, a glory-seeking attorney, Marty (played by Richard Gere), defends a young man, Aaron (played by Edward Norton), against charges of murdering a priest. He does this because, as he says, "I choose to believe in that basic goodness of people. I choose to believe that not all crimes are committed by bad people. And I try to understand that some very, very good people do some very bad things."

Marty "proves" in a court of law that the murderer has multiple personalities and is therefore not guilty of his crime. Afterward, Marty meets with Aaron, now being transferred to a psychiatric hospital, and Aaron reveals to Marty that he faked the multiple personalities in order to get away with the crime. Marty walks away in defeat because his humanistic belief in the goodness of humanity blinded him to the real evil right in front of him. In this case, as in the others, the criminal getting away with the crime is intended to be a warning to the rest of us to follow righteousness and avoid compromise with evil, or else evil will triumph.

Sometimes stories in which people do the right thing are not desirable because of the context of the decision. The context can turn what is otherwise good moral behavior into ultimately immoral values. *The Bridges of Madison County* (1995)—the tear-jerking romance adapted by Richard LaGravenese from Robert James Waller's popular novel—is the story of a small-town married woman (played by Meryl Streep) who has a short adulterous affair with a dashing, globe-trotting photographer for *National Geographic* (played by Clint Eastwood). She feels the stultifying pressure of her traditional role as mother and wife and is tempted to leave her family behind to remain with this fast-living man of the world. At the end she chooses the right thing—to stay with her family and husband. She realizes that the fantasy will not deliver the ultimate romantic satisfaction she longs for any more than does her current situation. Here is a story that accepts the covenant a woman has made with her spouse and children as a higher responsibility than the fleeting effect of hormones.

The downside of this portrayal is that the woman never confesses to her husband and clings to her tryst of infidelity all her life as her one true experience of real love, in contrast to her boring, conventional married life. Rather than rekindling lost love in her flesh-and-blood husband, she retreats psychologically into her fantasy of unfaithfulness. This movie proposes doing the moral thing on the surface, but its context encourages immorality of the heart: romantic fantasy as emotional pornography.

Drawing the Balance

By differentiating between exploitation and exhortation, the greatest story ever told expresses standards of morality without compromising its honesty about the human condition. However, after trying to establish some guidelines for the definition of exploitation, we must face the reality that the lines will not be the same for everyone. What is exploitation for one person is often moral exhortation for another. This is not to say that all morality is relative. But it *is* to say that we should discuss our opinions with others in an open dialogue and with enough humility to recognize when we may be wrong—and to change our views, if needed. One of the purposes of the arts is to stimulate discussion of values and beliefs, to engage in soul-searching discourse with one another.

Leland Ryken's *The Liberated Imagination* does a great job of helping the adult individual understand the nature of modern art and guiding adults to draw their own lines of balance. On the difficulty of dealing with realism in the arts and biblical allowance, he concludes,

Whenever we find ourselves wondering about the legitimacy of Christian contact with modern art, we should stop to consider that we cannot run away from our own society, that we must face its art and values, and that the Bible itself insists on our contact with realism in art. We are left walking a tightrope between the extremes of total rejection and total affirmation.

A sense of balance is what a Christian needs. People who are inclined either to immerse themselves in modern art or to avoid it completely probably need to check their inclination.[13]

Christians tend to be either cultural gluttons or cultural anorexics. It seems we either avoid all movies or watch too many of them. We must be honest enough to face our selfish tendency to rationalize our own prejudices. As pointed out earlier, one person's sense of exploitation may simply illustrate his own prudery, while another person's tolerance may actually be her own indulgence in besetting sin. Hopefully, through the exchange of opinions with an open mind and a humble disposition, we can use movies and their contrast of humanity's lighter and darker sides as a means of understanding and interacting redemptively with ourselves and the world around us.

---

[13]Leland Ryken, *The Liberated Imagination: Thinking Christianly About the Arts* (Wheaton, Ill.: Harold Shaw, 1989), pp. 255-56.